THE JAPANESE SENTENCE

AN INTRODUCTION TO JAPANESE GRAMMAR

THE JAPANESE SENTENCE

AN INTRODUCTION TO JAPANESE GRAMMAR

Hugh Stewart

Japan is One Nation

One Civilization

One Language

One Culture

One Race

This work is dedicated to

My many friends in Ota ku, Tokyo
and elsewhere in Japan,

My many friends who participated in the WISH
program at Salem State University,

My sensei Reiko Asahina Marcos,
who encouraged me to write this book,

and
My wife Yoko,
an excellent assistant
and a wonderful companion.

Preface

My first interest in things Japanese began when my uncle Kermit Stewart returned from a long tour in Japan following World War II. While there he studied Japanese and, incidentally, was the first *gaijin* (non-Japanese) to conduct the Tokyo Symphony Orchestra after the war.

He taught me to count to ten in Japanese. That was a tiny seed. After retiring from a career of electronic engineering and computer programming, I read Clavell's "Shogun" and learned another bit of Japanese language along with *Anjin san*, the hero of the story.

I discovered that Asian students at nearby Salem State University had little exposure to American home life, and started project that I called WISH, for Welcome International Students to our Homes. I met and became friends with many Japanese students.

My then wife, a docent at the Peabody Essex Museum in Salem Massachusetts, got an opportunity for us to tour Japan as members of the Salem Ota Cultural Exchange. Salem is the sister city of Ota- ku, a city in Tokyo Metropolis. Following that wonderful tour, my interest in all things Japanese, including the language, soared. I found a sensei and began learning the language. I made three more trips to Japan and my friendships with Ota residents grew stronger.

After my late wife lost a battle with cancer I decided, at the ripe age of 82, to pack up and move to Tokyo to study the language. Poor vision forced me to abandon school. But my interest in the language continued. I stayed in Japan for two years, served as an international goodwill ambassador for the city of Ota-ku, and there met my future wife. I continued to study the Japanese language on my own.

At first it seemed to be a bunch of assorted rules for putting together a sentence. But my engineering mind started to see how things were related, and to organize the various rules into a logical plan. Over time I evolved a model that gave structure to the grammar. It is the basis for this book. As an engineer, I crave order and logic. Where English is a mishmash of words and structures from many cultures, the Japanese evolved in a closed world and is consistent. I found the grammar to be much simpler than the way it is taught.

Although the model presented here is unique, it is not the only model of Japanese grammar. Curé Dolly, who purports to be a *Meiji* era doll that gained human traits, has a series on YouTube and some books describing a model. I find her train analogy a bit too cute, and one must endure her persistent criticism of traditional teaching. But she is a rare find for explaining the why of various grammar points, which is otherwise difficult to find. Another model is by Richard Webb, in his book 80/20 Japanese. Both Dolly and Webb go into greater depth and are recommended if you want to pursue the language.

Almost all my research has been on the web. One notable source is I found is Michiel Kamerman's "An Introduction to Japanese Syntax, Grammar, and Language," that clarified some points that had bothered me.

I thank Reiko Asahina Marcos for encouraging me to write this book. Marcos is a university teacher of Japanese and was my *sensei* for many years.

And special thanks to my wife Yoko for serving as a sounding board for my ideas and correcting my many errors.

Hugh Stewart
Marblehead, Massachusetts, USA
June 2022

Have a comment? Please feel free to send corrections, criticisms, or kudos to Author@jsentence.com.

Table of Contents

INTRODUCTION

A CHILD BEGINS LEARNING ITS NATIVE LANGUAGE AS SOON AS IT IS BORN. It does not learn about nouns and verbs and other grammatical structures, it simply learns – in time - how to construct sentences and communicate. Perhaps in middle school years it finally learns the terms of grammar.

Learning a new language as a grown person is not the same. Some lucky few learn by immersion into a community of speakers of the language, but most study books and/or attend classes. Various teaching methods are used: flash cards to build vocabulary, text, or lectures to learn the components of the language and how to use them in building or understanding sentences.

The rules of the Japanese language are more structured than most languages. This is the result of Japanese isolation for thousands of years. While English is a hodgepodge of many languages, there were no outside influences on the development of Japanese. Yet we teach the languages in formats that do not reveal the structure. The result is the appearance of a difficult language to learn.

Granted, learning to read Japanese, with *kanji* and *kana* characters to learn, can be daunting. And counting in Japanese is not simple; _for_ instance, we say three sheets of paper or five quarts of water. Sheets and quarts are counter words. We also say two houses or nine pigs, with no counter word. But Japanese always use a counter, so it is *ni ken no ie* ([counter] of houses) and *kyu tou no buta* (nine heads of pigs). And the days of the month (first, second, ...) are from before the West introduced weeks, so are based on the Lunar Calendar: *tsuitachi, futsuka, mikka, yokka, ...).* But there is no need to add to the complexity with grammar rules that do not make sense.

About this book

This book presents the basic grammar of Japanese in an orderly format. It is easy to read and absorb. It provides beginners a sense of structure into which future learning fits. It helps the advanced student to organize what is already learned. It is an invaluable addition to any student's studies.

It is my hope that this model will be helpful to those venturing into the language of Japan, and that others will refine and build on this model to make it more accurate and yet keep it simple so that it continues to be a useful tool for understanding Japanese.

About this text

Although many Japanese words will be used, they are to illustrate grammar concepts; vocabulary is not the object of this book. All Japanese words are presented in *Romaji*. This is because I have no idea what level of Japanese you can read. Whether you read full Japanese easily or not at all, you are reading this text, so you are able to read *Romaji*.

Many teachers object to this approach, saying you should learn to read, speak, and listen at the same time. I do not want to leave anyone out. Even if you are only interested in conversational Japanese, I want you to be able to read this.

In this book we have chosen the following:

All Japanese is written in *Romaji* and italicized.

Many words are unsaid in Japanese. Where this occurs, the missing words are enclosed in parentheses in the translation.

Except for topics, translation is word-for-word. That means the order is often strange to western ears.

<u>Example</u>

watashi	*wa,*	*(watashi)*	*(ga)*	*kinō*	*Kōbe*	*ni*	*iki*	*mashita.*
As for me,		(I)		yesterday	Kōbe to		go	did
Topic Element		Subject Element		Adverb Element	Adverb Element		Verb Element	

Yesterday I went to Kōbe

When the meaning does not seem obvious, the natural English interpretation is shown below. The sentence is "As for me, yesterday *Kōbe* to go did". Too often, textbooks only tell you the sentence is "Yesterday I went to Kōbe. That does not help you learn.

About the Model

The linguist community has names for parts of speech that are often mysterious to us laypeople. I have taken the liberty of changing the names of some items. I have adopted terms that I think will be more readily understood.

Traditional	**Model**	**Traditional**	**Model**
Imperative	Command	*na* Adjective	Noun-adj
Causative	Cause-Let	*i* Adjective	Adjective
Desire	Want	Auxiliary	Key
Hypothetical	If-Then	Suffix	Tail
Passive	Receiving	Conjugation	Formation
Potential	Able-to	Progressive	On-going

In this model, verbs and adjectives never change (except for two irregular verbs). They have a separate tail that changes with the form:

Verb	Tail
Adjective	Tail

For instance, *ki* is a verb, *kiku* is the Dictionary form with the tail *ku*.

The model includes copulas, which are not always familiar to students. It never mentions transitive/intransitive verbs, although Japanese students learn these forms instead of copulas.

This book is in two parts:

Japan, presenting a brief history of Japan and its language, discussion of the spoken and written language and the influence of culture on the language, and

Grammar, presenting Japanese grammar in the form of a model identifying types of words, phrases, sentence elements, and sentences.

PART 1 – JAPAN

Chapter 1-1
JAPANESE HISTORY

THE FIRST PEOPLES TO INHABIT THE ISLANDS NOW CALLED JAPAN arrived about 35,000 years ago. They were stone-age hunter-gatherers living is small family groups. At that time, Japan was part of Asia. The Sea of Japan (East Sea) was a large lake, and people could walk around it to arrive in Japan. About 14,000 years ago, global warming brought an end to the ice age, and the melting ice raised the oceans, separating Japan from the mainland.

Jomon Culture

Around 10,000 years ago, humans began arriving via land bridges from Asia, although just where they came from is a mystery. Called the *Jomon]* people, they were hunter-gatherers. Although they created villages, they were not farmers. Homes were generally pits dug in the ground and covered with a thatch roof. They seem to have lived peacefully – the archaeological evidence shows no signs of violent deaths. They independently developed the bow and arrow for hunting animals, and pottery. The latter was unique, with elaborate designs. The *Jomon* name comes from the decoration of pots by pressing rope into the clay before firing.

By 300 BCE, they were suffering; they had used up most of the natural resources – plants and wild animals – and their population was declining. Japanese mythology has the first emperor descending from the sun goddess in 660 BCE, beginning the current line of emperors.

Since they had no written language, we know almost nothing of their speech.

Yayoi Culture

Wet rice farming was developed around 4500 BCE in the Yangtse river valley in China, and rapidly spread throughout Asia.

Around 300 BCE (some say as early as early as 800 or 900 BCE) new peoples began arriving in Japan. Again, their origin is a subject for debate. They are called *Yayois*, for the section of Tokyo where the first archeological evidence of their existence was discovered. The *Yayois* brought with them mining and processing of bronze and iron, new pottery styles, and wet rice faming. They took over – the *Jomon* peoples disappeared, either assimilated or exterminated by the *Yayois*.

Wet rice farming requires large numbers of people and structured society: they must prepare fields, plant, wed, harvest, store, and distribute the rice. The *Yayois* lived in villages. Village leaders evolved into chiefs, and chiefs united into confederations that ultimately led to the modern state. Frequent wars occurred as chiefs attempted to increase their land or crop failures caused one village to raid another for food. The elements of the Shinto religion developed as people prayed for good crops and good babies.

Since there was no written language, the language of the *Yayoi* is little known but is most likely the origin of modern Japanese.

Trade with China began in the 6th century CE. Much of what we know about the *Yayois* came from writing by Chinese visitors. In time, scholars began using Chinese characters, and from those writings linguists get some clues about the origin of the language. Some believe it has roots in the Austronesian or Malaya-Polynesian languages. This is based in part on the fact that they share the same five vowels. However, Japanese originally had eight vowels, so that pretty much dismisses that idea. Others believe Japanese originated with Altaic family of Turkic, Mongolic and Tungusic languages. However, the Altaic theory is now largely dismissed.

Today it is largely believed to have originated with ancient Korean. Both have postposition- as opposed to prepositions - and neither have articles (the, a, *etc.*). And they sound similar. Most linguists now believe that the language was brought to Japan from the Korean peninsula around 700 to 300 BCE by wet- rice farmers of the *Yayoi* culture and spread throughout the Japanese archipelago, replacing Indigenous languages.

Kafun Period

The period from 300 CE to 352 CE is called the *Kafun* (old tombs) era. Giant tombs were created for rulers - covering as much as 80 acres (32 hectares) of land. These tombs show that the rulers had grown to have great power. In this period Japanese elite used Chinese forms for writing.

Yamato Period

From 352 CE to 710 CE, the *Yamatos* ruled Japan. *Yamato* was a confederation of chiefs. The *Yamato* society was organized into clans, whose chiefs claimed descent directly from the Sun Goddess *Amaterasu*. They used religious symbols, military might, and intermarriages to extend their power to much of Japan.

The first contact between China and Japan occurred during the Chinese Sui dynasty (561-618 CE). There being no writing method for Japanese, scholars began using Chinese writing.

In a letter to the ruler of China in 607 CE, the Japanese spoke of the sun rising in Japan and setting in China. The Chinese felt insulted by this little immature country calling itself an empire, and by being called the land of the setting sun. However, the idea of the land of the rising sun took hold and in time became Japan's name – *Nihon* (or *Nippon*) – sun's origin. The name Japan probably comes from the Portuguese corruption of an early Chinese name for the country – *Cipangu*.

Nara Period

The *Nara* period, 710-814 CE, followed the *Yamata* period. This saw the establishment of the first permanent capital at *Nara*, the development of administrative institutions, and the beginning of the classical period.

In that era, the Japanese language had eight vowels.

During the Chinese Tang dynasty (618-907 CE), contact with China was again established. Buddhism was introduced.

The use of Chinese writing was very difficult, because Chinese is very different from Japanese. Soon, Japanese scholars adopted a style called *man'yōgana,* in which Chinese characters (which the Japanese call *kanji*) were used both for meaning and for sounds. For instance, *tabe masu* might be written as the Chinese character for eat – *tabe* (食)– and Chinese characters pronounced ma (那) and su (寸), resulting in 食那寸 [There are many kanji for each of these sounds – the ones shown here were picked at random]. The reader had to determine whether each character was to be read for its meaning or its sound – not an easy task.

The solution was the creation of a set of characters representing sounds. Called *kana*, it is traditionally said to have been invented by the Buddhist priest *Kūkai* in the 9th century. On his return from China in 806 CE; his interest in the sacred aspects of speech and writing led him to the conclusion that Japanese would be better represented by a phonetic alphabet. His contribution is called *kana*.

The Heian Period

The *Heian* period extended to 1185 CE. The capital was moved to Kyoto. It was a time of splendid classical Japanese culture. In those days, women were not allowed to learn *kanji*. So *hira gana* was invented for their use. *Hira gana* has the same characters as *kata kana* but drawn differently. It is sort of like print and script in English. The court, - especially women – created great poetry, diaries, and the novel 'Tale of Genji'".

The number of vowels was reduced from eight to today's five, and long and short vowels and consonants were introduced.

Medieval Period

Military rule came into being during this time. The new *samurai* class replaced the nobility as the rulers of Japan. The Imperial court remained in *Kyoto*, while the *Shogun* government was in *Kamakura*. Although artistry flourished, this period was one of continuous wars.

Contact with China resumed during the Ming dynasty (1368-1644 CE). The Chinese dialect was different during each of the three periods of contact. As a result, many *kanji* have more than one reding, adopted from the different periods.

In 1543, the first Europeans arrived in Japan. They were Portuguese, intent of trade and on spreading Catholicism. They introduced a number of 'loan' words into Japanese, such as *pan* (bread), *koppu* (cup). *kōhī* (coffee), and *gurasu* (glass).

Throughout the *Heian* and Medieval periods, the language continued to evolve toward today's modern Japanese.

Edo Period

1603 CE began the Early Modern Japan era. The *Tokugawa* family seized power in that year and began 264 years as *Shoguns*, leaving the Emperor with only spiritual duties. Called the *Edo* period, the *Shogun* required all *Daimyos* to keep their families in the new capital *Edo* - later to be renamed *Tokyo*. The families were essentially hostages to prevent the *Daimyos* from starting a war. The result was a quarter-century of peace. *Samurais* turned to art as a pastime, and poetry, painting, and other art forms flourished anew.

Soon after taking power, the *Shogun* banned Catholicism. All European Catholics were driven out or killed; Japanese Catholics were forced to renounce Catholicism or die. Only a handful of Protestant Dutch was allowed to trade - they were restricted to *De Jima* - a small artificial island in *Nagasaki*.

Bot the Portuguese and Dutch made contributions to the Japanese language – new words were 'borrowed.' The Europeans also brought muskets, quickly changing the way wars were fought.

The *Shogunate* adopted Neo-Confucianism. This led to a class structure - samurai, food producers, artisans, and merchants. The *samurai* were the rulers as the armies of the *Daimyos*. Their power was such that they could decapitate any who offended them. They obeyed their respective *Daimyos*, who in turn obeyed the *Shogun*. The Emperor was merely the spiritual leader with no secular power.

By Confucian standards, farmers and fishermen were high in status because they produced the most necessary thing - food. Artisans came next because they also produced things that were needed – clothing, pottery, swords, decorative items, *etc.* Merchants were at the bottom because they created nothing but got money for distributing other people's creations.

Meiji Restoration

In 1857, the American Navy threatened *Tokyo* with bombardment from its ships, and the government agreed to open the doors. Soon after that, the *Shogun* stepped down and Emperor *Meiji* was restored to full power.

1864 CE marked the beginning of modern Japan. The *Meiji* restoration changed Japan completely. The *Meiji* court abolished the class system and avidly adopted western ways - from clothing to technology.

The *Meiji* government established a national dialect based on that spoken in the higher-class areas of *Tokyo.* Today there are still regions of Japan with their own dialect – some so different that they are not readily understood by mainstream Japanese.

Western influence introduced *Romaji*, spelling Japanese words with Roman (English) letters.

Several wars followed as Japan grew in international stature. Finally, for many reasons, the country took on the western nations of the United States, England, France, *etc.* Overwhelmed by technology and logistics, the war was lost in 1945.

Postwar Era

The war's end marked the beginning of the contemporary era for Japan. The country was devastated. Most cities had been reduced to rubble by American bombing. The United States and other Allies helped build a new Japan. Under U.S. occupation, a new constitution was developed that, among other features, forbade Japan from fighting other nations.

In 1946, the government declared that 1,850 *kanji* characters were official, and publishers should attempt to limit their printing to those characters. Today the official count is 2,136 *kanji* characters. Despite the complexity of *kanji* with *hiragana*, *katakana*, and *Romaji*, Japan has one of the world's highest literacy rates.

From 1511 to 1634, *Kyoto* was the third-largest city in the world, after Beijing and Istanbul. After the *Shogunate* moved to *Edo* (now *Tokyo*) that city became #3 in 1634, and in 1954 moved to #1, where it remains today. (Technically, *Tokyo* is a Metropolis – a special category of prefecture or state, comprised of 23 cities and several commuter towns).

Although *katakana* was favored for almost all non-*kanji* writing, around 1950 *hiragana* was designated as the standard for Japanese words, and *katakana* for all words and names 'borrowed' from other languages. And there are many. After the *Meiji* restoration, a flood of technical and other foreign words, chiefly from English, but also from French and German, became part of the language. Many words like *kompyūta* (computer), *esukareta* (escalator), and *disku* (disk) have entered the vocabulary of Japan.

In 1940, there were almost no non-native speakers of Japanese in the United States. Today, it is a popular language to learn. There are some 140 million native speakers of Japanese, making it the ninth most used language.

Because Japan was isolated for almost its entire history, except for the introduction of Chinese characters and words, there is very little outside influence in the language –the grammar is unique and not directly traceable to any other language. And it is very structured, especially when compared with English, which is a conglomeration of many languages and has relatively little consistency.

Chapter 1-2

SPOKEN JAPANESE

THERE IS A SPECIFIC SET OF SOUNDS used in Japanese speech. Each is either a vowel sound, or a combination of a consonant and vowel, plus the sound of the letter n. The good news is any given sound is always said the same way. There is no "I see the bird, you saw it". In Japanese if you see the spelling in *kana,* or *Romaji,* you know how to pronounce it.

<table>
<tr><td></td><td colspan="5" align="center">Vowels</td><td colspan="3" align="center">Combinations</td></tr>
<tr><td></td><td>a</td><td>i</td><td>u</td><td>e</td><td>o</td><td>*va*</td><td>*vi*</td><td>*ve*</td></tr>
<tr><td>k</td><td>*ka*</td><td>*ki*</td><td>*ku*</td><td>*ke*</td><td>*ko*</td><td>*kya*</td><td>*kyu*</td><td>*kyo*</td></tr>
<tr><td>g</td><td>*ga*</td><td>*gi*</td><td>*gu*</td><td>*ge*</td><td>*go*</td><td></td><td></td><td></td></tr>
<tr><td>s</td><td>*sa*</td><td>*shi*</td><td>*su*</td><td>*se*</td><td>*so*</td><td>*sha*</td><td>*shu*</td><td>*sho*</td></tr>
<tr><td>z</td><td>*za*</td><td>*zi*</td><td>*zu*</td><td>*ze*</td><td>*zo*</td><td></td><td></td><td></td></tr>
<tr><td>t</td><td>*ta*</td><td>*chi*</td><td>*tsu*</td><td>*te*</td><td>*to*</td><td>*cha*</td><td>*chu*</td><td>*cho*</td></tr>
<tr><td>d</td><td>*da*</td><td>*di*</td><td>*du*</td><td>*de*</td><td>*do*</td><td></td><td></td><td></td></tr>
<tr><td>n</td><td>*na*</td><td>*ni*</td><td>*nu*</td><td>*ne*</td><td>*no*</td><td>*nya*</td><td>*nyu*</td><td>*nyo*</td></tr>
<tr><td>h</td><td>*ha*</td><td>*hi*</td><td>*hu*</td><td>*he*</td><td>*ho*</td><td>*hya*</td><td>*hyu*</td><td>*hyo*</td></tr>
<tr><td>b</td><td>*ba*</td><td>*bi*</td><td>*bu*</td><td>*be*</td><td>*bo*</td><td>*fa*</td><td>*fi*</td><td>*fe*</td></tr>
<tr><td>p</td><td>*pa*</td><td>*pi*</td><td>*pu*</td><td>*pe*</td><td>*po*</td><td></td><td></td><td></td></tr>
<tr><td>m</td><td>*ma*</td><td>*mi*</td><td>*mu*</td><td>*me*</td><td>*mo*</td><td>*mya*</td><td>*myu*</td><td>*myo*</td></tr>
<tr><td>y</td><td>*ya*</td><td></td><td>*yu*</td><td></td><td>*yo*</td><td></td><td></td><td></td></tr>
<tr><td>r</td><td>*ra*</td><td>*ri*</td><td>*ru*</td><td>*re*</td><td>*ro*</td><td>*rya*</td><td>*ryu*</td><td>*ryo*</td></tr>
<tr><td>w</td><td>*wa*</td><td>*wi*</td><td></td><td>*we*</td><td>*wo*</td><td></td><td></td><td></td></tr>
<tr><td>n</td><td colspan="5" align="center">*n*</td><td></td><td></td><td></td></tr>
</table>

(Consonants — row label at left side of the Vowels table)

Of course, it is not that easy. There are long and short vowels, double consonants, and silent characters. And within Japan, there are several dialects that sound quite different. The usage cited herein is generally that heard in Tokyo, which is considered standard Japanese.

Vowels

There are five vowels in the Japanese language. They are the top row of the preceding table: *a, i, u, e, o.* Vowels can be short or long, but not in the English sense. There are various ways to write a long vowel in Romaji; one is to place a bar over it (ā *ī ū ē ō*); another is to repeat each long vowel (*aa, ii, uu, ee, oo*).

Consider the words *oki* and *ōkii.* In the first case, the sound of *o* and *i* are short. If you spoke *oki* with a metronome, it would take a count of two - *o* and *ki.*

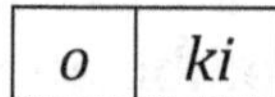

But *ōkii* would take a count of four (two for *ō*, one for *ki*, one for the final *i*).

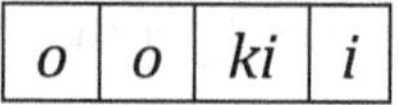

These are totally different words - *oki* means several different things - one is 'offshore' - while *ō,kii* means 'big.' Yet the only difference is in their pronunciation is in the length of the vowels (the *kanji* characters are very different).

Long vowels are said smoothly. You don't say o o, you say o- as one sound but held longer. Think of lot and loot. A long vowel is displayed in Romaji in various ways. With *hiragana*, the vowel is written two times: いい (*ii*). The character long o is usually written in Romaji as *ou* (おう). With *katakana*, a long vowel is followed by a dash: o— (オー). And with Romaji it is usually written with a bar over each long vowel (*ō*) or a double letter (*oo*) or (*ou*).

The vowels *i* and *u* are not always sounded. For instance, the common word *desu* and *masu* are often pronounced *des'* and *mas'* respectively. Similarly, the verb ending *mashita* is usually pronounced *mash'ta.* In each case, although no sound is made, the timing is as if the sound is made, and the mouth should be shaped as if it were making the sound. Of course, you will also hear *desu* and *masu*, it is like "you say tomato and I say tomahto".

Consonants

The consonants are *k g, s, j, z, t, d, n, h, b, p, m, y, r, and w.* Note that *y* is considered to be a consonant. Notice also that there is no character for the sound of v, q, l, or c (except as k). These sounds do not occur in Japanese speech When using foreign words, r is usually used in place of l – and b in place of v. Thus, elevator is said *erebēt*□ (ay ray bay tah). A sound that is not in English is *tsu.* It sounds like the *ts* in cats plus *u* as in you. Think of *tsunami.*

Most consonants are pronounced the same as in English. Two exceptions are *g* and *r*. When it occurs in the middle of a word, *g* is pronounced more like *ng*, as in ring. *r* is pronounced more like d – the tongue should touch the roof of the mouth when sounding r.

Consonants may also be stretched but are represented differently from vowels. With *hiragana*, a small *tsu* (つ) character indicates that the following consonant should be stretched- がっこう (*ga**kk**ō*), while *katakana* uses a dash to stretch the preceding character:ガッコー. With Romaji, printing the letter twice indicates that it is stretched: ***gakkō*** .

In English, we say, '**a** thing' and '**an** old thing.' Why is that? Just because 'an thing' and 'a old thing' do not roll off the tongue so easily. Japanese has a similar situation; some words are spelled with alternate characters for ease of speech. These are the sounds represented with the *tenten* (") or *maru* (o) in the *kana* alphabet, which we will visit in the next chapter. They are:

Character	Alternate	Examples
kか	g が	*kawa/gawa* (river)
sさ	z ざ	*sake/zake* (alcohol)
tた	d だ	*da/ta* (rice field)
hは	b ぱ	*hito/bito* (person)
hは	p ぱ	*hon/pon* (book)

That is why we say *hira**g**ana* and *kata**k**ana.; gana* and *kana* mean the same word – *hira**k**ana* or *kata**g**ana* are not so pleasant sounding. And you are free to call the country *Ni**h**on* or *Ni**pp**on.*

This dissertation is an introduction – there are many subtle points that a student can study after reading this.

Chapter 1-3
WRITTEN JAPANESE

WRITTEN JAPANESE USES FOUR SETS OF CHARACTERS. The basic set is *kanji:* Chinese characters that represent nouns, verbs, and adjectives. *kana* characters are used for Japanese words for which there is no *kanji,* and to supplement *kanji* words. There are two forms of *kana; hiragana is* used for Japanese, and *katakana* is used for foreign words. Finally, *Romaji* – Japanese words spelled with English letters - is used, usually for company or brand names.

As recently as the middle of the 20th century, *katakana* was used for Japanese words. Then the government changed it. Today, Japanese words and *kanji* endings are written with *hiragana,* and foreign words and names are written with *katakana.*

Kanji

Kanji characters represent full words or word bases. They were borrowed from China as the earliest form of writing. *Kanji* characters are comprised of two to over twenty strokes. Most *kanji* have two types of readings - ways to say the character. One is called the *On* reading and is the original Chinese sound of the character; the other is the *Kun* reading, which is the Japanese pronunciation. For example, 車 means vehicle. the O*n* reading is *sha,* and the *kun* reading is *kuruma.* You can see these in the Japanese words for bicycle - *jitensha* and automobile – *kuruma.*

Often there is more than one *On* or *Kun* reading. For instance, 生 has two *On* readings *(sē, shō),* and twenty-five *kun* readings *(asa, iki, iku, ike, ubu, umai, e, oi, gyū, kurumi, gose, sa, jō, sugi, so, sō, chiru, naba, niu, nyū, fu, mi, mō, yoi, and ryū).* There are tens of thousands of *kanji* characters, most of which are very rarely used. 2,000 to 3,000 are in common use in Japan. The government has identified about 2,000 to be taught in schools.

A study of one year of printing in a newspaper revealed the following:

Number of kanji	Frequency
100	40%
200	57%
500	80%
1,000	98%
2,000	99.7%
3,000	99,97%

If you know the 500 most used *kanji*, you could read 80% of the text.

Most *kanji* characters used in the Japanese language are over 400 years old, and many are much older. In 1950, the Chinese government adopted a set of simplified characters. The Japanese still use the old original characters. As a result, a Chinese person today may not be able to recognize all of the *kanji* used in Japan, and Japanese people cannot read modern Chinese writing.

Kana

There are two-character sets created by the Japanese: *hiragana* and *katakana*. *Hiragana* is used for particles, verb auxiliaries, and other words for which there is no *kanji* character. *Katakana* is used for words borrowed from other languages, foreign words, some emotional words, some slang, and onomatopoeia (*e.g., pikapika*).

When Chinese writing was first used, it was recognized that it did not allow for all the nuances of spoken Japanese. For instance, a Japanese verb can have many auxiliaries. The verb 'eat' can be used for 'eating,' 'ate,' 'did not eat,' 'let's eat,' and many more. The *kanji* character is simply 'eat.' *kana* was invented to solve this problem. *Hiragana* words are appended to the *kanji* character to change the form of the verb phrase. For instance, *mashita* (ました.in *hiragana)* can be appended to the *kanji* character for 'eat' (食) to make the past tense 'ate':食べ ました.

Every Japanese word can be written with *kana* characters. However, because there are relatively few sounds in Japanese, there are many homonyms. Just hearing a word does not always tell you what word is being used. But the *kanji* character for each word is different. Using the *kanji* character, possibly supplemented by the *kana* characters, is unambiguous. As an example, *kyūyō* - means 'recreation' and also 'urgent business. If you encountered it in *kana* alone, you might not know which meaning to use. The *kanji* characters are very different (休養 and 急用), so using *kanji* removes the ambiguity.

Hiragana and *katakana* have the same characters drawn differently. *Katakana* is comprised of mostly straight lines, while *hiragana* is more rounded. It is analogous to English block printing and *script*.

The table below shows all the *kana* characters. Pronunciation of each character is row name followed by column name. For instance, the third row (g), and the third column (u), contains the character *gu* (ぐ). Exceptions are *si->shi, ti->chi, tu->tsu*

Hiragana

	a	i	u	e	o	
	あ	い	う	え	お	
k	か	き	く	け	こ	
g	が	ぎ	ぐ	げ	ご	*tenten*
s	さ	し	す	せ	そ	
z	ざ	じ	ず	ぜ	ぞ	*tenten*
t	た	ち	つ	て	と	
d	だ	ぢ	づ	で	ど	*tenten*
n	な	に	ぬ	ね	の	
h	は	ひ	ふ	へ	ほ	
b	ば	び	ぶ	べ	ぼ	*tenten*
p	ぱ	ぴ	ぷ	ぺ	ぽ	*maru*
m	ま	み	む	め	も	
y	や		ゆ		よ	
r	ら	り	る	れ	ろ	
w	わ	ゐ		ゑ	を	
	ん (n)					

Katakana

	a	i	u	e	o
	ア	イ	ウ	エ	オ
k	カ	キ	ク	ケ	コ
g	ガ	ギ	グ	ゲ	ゴ
s	タ	チ	ツ	テ	ト
z	ザ	ジ	ズ	ゼ	ゾ
t	ハ	ヒ	フ	ヘ	ホ
d	ダ	チ "	ヅ	デ	ド
n	ナ	ニ	ヌ	ネ	ノ
h	ラ	リ	ル	レ	ロ
b	バ	ビ	ブ	ベ	ボ
p	パ	ピ	ぷ	ペ	ポ
m	ア	イ	ウ	エ	オ
y	カ	キ	ク	ケ	コ
r	サ	シ	ス	セ	ソ
w	タ	チ	ツ	テ	ト
	ナ (n)				

*ten**ten** and maru*

Some *kana* characters have a little symbol, something like a double quote (")
next to them. It is called a *tenten* and changes the consonant from one sound
to another. Characters beginning with *h* can have a small circle, similar to the
symbol for temperature (°); it is called a *maru*, and changes the sound *h* to *p*.

k"	is pronounced	g	*kawa/gawa*
s"	is pronounced	z	*sake/zake*
t"	is pronounced	d	*non te/non de*
h"	is pronounced	b	*hito/bito*
h°	is pronounced	p	*Nihon/Nippon*

Romaji

Romaji is simply sounding out text with Roman (English) characters. It has
become common practice for company and brand names, in order to sell to a
foreign market. Subaru, Sony, Canon, and Mitsubishi are examples of the use
of *Romaji*.

It is possible to have all types of character in one sentence:

Sony は,アメリカの<u>市場</u>を <u>持</u>ってるています。
As for Sony, (it) American market has
i.e., Sony has a market in America.

The <u>under-lined</u> characters are *kanji*, the **bold** characters are *katakana*, Sony is
Romaji, the rest are *hiragana*.

We should also mention *furigana*. It is simply *kanji* with tiny *hiragana* spelling
of the word appearing over the *kanji*. This is used for those who cannot read
kanji, and for teaching *kanji*.

Writing Direction

Printed Japanese can be in either of two formats: vertical or
horizontal. Vertical printing has the characters begin top right
and go down, continuing in a new column to the left. For centuries
this was the basic way Japanese (and Chinese) has been written.
It originated with writing on scrolls, using the right hand to brush
the text and the left hand to unroll and feed the scroll. It is still

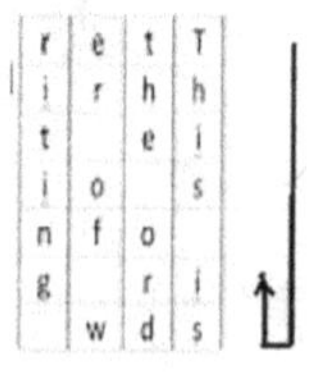

used today. Books printed in this form open from what Westerners consider the back, with the spine on the right.

Vertically printed Japanese does not have spaces between words. When written horizontally, there is often a space after a particle (you will understand later), especially after a comma or period. It is argued that the *kanji* in the words will help to know where a word begins. If the text is all *kana*, that does not work so well. Children's books often include spaces between every word.

Punctuation

Commas did not come into use until the *Meiji* period when Western influence took hold. There are no formal rules for how to use them. Punctuation marks are shown here.

、	comma
。	period
「 」	open and close quote
『 』	open and close double quote
々	repeat for kanji

Quote symbols are rotated 90 degrees for vertical writing. Double quotes are used for book titles, names, *etc.*

Drawing kanji

The order in which strokes are made is considered very important. Continually following the rules helps build a memory that in turn helps to remember each character.

Drawing works top to bottom, left to right. If there is a long vertical line that does not protrude a bottom line, it is drawn first; otherwise, it is drawn after all the intersecting horizontal lines. Crossing diagonals are drawn top right to bottom left first. Containers are drawn before the contents. For compound *kanji* each is drawn in order from top to bottom, left to right. These are the general rules; there are many more.

Today writing is often with a ballpoint pen; in earlier times a brush was used, and elegance was respected.

Reason for kanji

So, why do the Japanese continue to use such a complex system of writing? First, they are proud of their heritage and like to keep old ways alive. There is practical reason, as well. The rather limited number of sounds in the Japanese language results in many homophones – words that sound alike. You quickly learn that the *kanji* is different for each word. Consider these:

bow	舳	Front of boat
bow	○脚	'O'legs
bow	弩	For shooting arrows
bow	弓	Used with violin
bow	拝	Bend at waist
bow	飾	Fancy knot of ribbon

In Japanese, unless the word is modern, each has different *kanji*. So, there is one practical use for *kanji*. Of course, as in English, the context usually lets you know which meaning is intended. And that is the way with spoken Japanese.

Because the language has relatively few different sounds, many Japanese words have multiple meanings when said, but the *kanji* is different for each. Consider this (non-sense) sentence:

  With chop sticks (I) cannot walk the bridge, so on the bridge's edge (I) ran.

In *Romaji*, it looks like this:

  hashi o motte hashi no hashi o aruke masen hashi no hashi o hashi ri mashita

hashi means bridge, chopsticks, and edge, and *hashiru* means run.

Of course, the Japanese do not use *Romaji*. In *hiragana,* it looks like this:

はしをもってはしのはしをあるけませんのではしのはしをはしりました。

Hiragana is phonetic, so it is still not obvious what each *hashi* means. But bridge, chopsticks, edge, and run each have different *kanji,* so in Japanese it looks like this:

箸を持って橋の端を歩けませんので橋の端を走りました。
(hashi in *kanji* is underlined)

A Japanese reader has no problem knowing what each *hashi* means.

Complex as the written language is the literacy rate in Japan is 99%. The saying "if it ain't broke, don't fix it" seems applicable here.

Chapter 1-4
JAPANESE CULTURE

L ESS THAN TWO HUNDRED YEARS AGO, Japan was under the rule of the *samurai* class. To be disrespectful of a *samurai* could easily and instantly cost your life. When a *daimyo* - a regional warlord – or one of his lords was traveling through an area, commoners in his path would fall to their knees and press their heads to the ground in respect – and fear. Today most authors blamed the politeness of today's Japanese to the population density. That certainly has a part. It is highly likely, though, that it is the remnants of the not so long-ago days of the *samurai.*

Class System

Prior to the *Meiji* Restoration, the class system was very strong. All of life bent to the system. There were four basic levels of society:

> the ruling *samurai* class,
> the food providers – farmers and fishers,
> the artisans who made clothing, swords, pottery, *etc.*, and
> the merchants.

This followed Confucian teaching; those who produced the necessities ranked highest, after of course the rulers. The merchants produced nothing and were considered parasites, making money from the work of others.

Butchers, leather workers, prostitutes, people handling the dead, garbage and night soil collectors, *etc.,* were not even in the system and were shunned as spiritually contaminated. The aristocracy was above the system.

Disasters

Japan is a country with many disasters. It lives on a tectonic plate that is prone to earthquakes and volcanic eruptions and is located in the Pacific where it experiences typhoons and *tsunamis.* When disasters occur, the people need to help each other. The person that helps himself ahead of others is shunned, rejected by society The Japanese people have lived with these disasters for eons, and it has affected their culture. The result is a country in which the individual's concerns are for the group rather than the self. Thus, a child considers the school as important; an adult worker is worried about making the company a success rather than his/her status in the company.

Confucius

Confucius was a philosopher who lived in China around 500 BCE. His teachings included:

> Respect for others, especially elders and superiors
> The need to perform well in one's work.
> The sense that one should know one's place in the system.
> Doing one's duty in accordance with one's place in society
> The self is defined in terms of the others about the person.
> The self is unimportant - the group is everything.

Japanese are taught from the beginning to be part of a group, not an individual. These teaching are consistent with the need to identify oneself as part of a community. Harmony is of utmost importance, and disturbing it is a serious matter.

Confucianism was officially removed from school curriculums by the post-World War II Occupation Administration, and today few people associate his teaching with their behavior But this does not mean his teachings are forgotten: the excellent work ethic, a strong sense of family, orderly and polite lives, ability to endure hardships (including all manner of disasters), striving to live in harmony with one another, respect for elders and superiors, and the sense that the goals of the group override the goals of the individual, all come from Confucius' teaching. The Japanese are trained in the first three years of elementary school in ways consistent with Confucius' teaching.

The class structure led to standards of behavior. Several levels of language evolved - from the casual language used among friends and within families to a high court language. It is said that the first time the Emperor spoke by radio to the citizenry, his imperial language was difficult to understand by most people.

Class and Language

Although the class system was abolished during the *Meiji* restoration, remnants exist. The most obvious is the use today of two levels of language among most people. Formal language is used when speaking to a person who is superior to the speaker, and informal when the roles are reversed. A third level is honorific and is used when speaking to some very superior person.

Superiority

Who is superior? It is sometimes difficult to discern. One factor is age. As with most Asian countries, older people are respected and thus are treated as superior. Customers are superior to store clerks. Supervisors are superior to their subordinates. Teachers and parents are superior to their children.

Another Confucius teaching that reaches into the Japanese language is respect for elders. All people are addressed as (name) *san* or some other honorific. This includes family members – the words for mother and father, for instance, are *okasan* and *otōsan*, respectively. *San* is an honorific showing respect. So even children use respectful language when addressing their parents.

There are words used to express respect, such as *gozai masu* and *kudasai* (please give me). In some cases, several words become the same in the polite form: *iku* (go), *kuru* (come), and *iru* (be) all become *irassharu*. Similarly, *taberu* (eat) and *nomu* (drink) in the polite form are both *meshiagaru*.

Among equals, the degree to which the parties know each other is a factor – the more social distance between them, the more formal the speech.

The formal language has a more complex verb formation. One does not omit obvious words as they tend to do in less formal situations.

In speech, different wording is used according to the level of language. This, coupled with the need to deal with several alphabets - *kanji, hiragana,* and *katakana,* and *Romaji* - is a large part of the reason many believe Japanese is a very difficult language. On top of the complexity of Japanese writing, today every Japanese student learns English in middle school, although most do not learn spoken English very well, and many lose their English skill afterward due to lack of use.

When speaking formally, adding honorifics to nouns is appropriate. The letter *o* is an honorific applied to many nouns. For instance, one can speak of *osake* (alcohol), *otera* (temple), or *ocha* (tea). If the noun is of Chinese origin, *go* can be used as a prefix: cooked rice is *gohan*.

Confucius taught that the person is subservient to the group. This concept is very strong in Asian countries. While westerners strive for personal success and recognition, the Japanese avoid individual attention. Their goal is the success of whatever organization they are part of, be it a family, school, business, or other. There is a saying; the nail that sticks up is the one that gets hammered. When they attend American schools, Japanese students tend to not raise their hands to answer a question - that is acting as an individual and focusing attention on one's self. When I ask to take a picture of a Japanese student friend, he or she is likely to wave to friends to come to be in the picture. Salarymen (white collar workers) often work long hours - without extra pay - to achieve company goals.

This and other behaviors are instilled in the first few years of school. Students are responsible for maintaining the school cleanliness, scrubbing floors and cleaning windows, *etc.*, for serving and clearing up after lunch, and more. Most schools have no janitors. The students wear uniforms, so they identify with the school group.

If you listen to a conversation among Japanese, you will seldom hear *watashi* (I) or *anata* (you). Many textbooks tell the student to avoid the use of these words.

It goes much deeper than avoiding individuality. Just one example: the statement *watashi wa, ringo ga suki desu* is typically translated as 'I like apples'. But it is better translated as 'As for me, apples are likable.' The focus is taken off the individual. *suki* and many other words shift the focus away from the speaker.

An ancient superstition throughout Asia is an avoidance of any reference to death. It shows up in numbers. Four is pronounced *shi*, which is the same sounding word as death. And seven is *shichi*. To avoid speaking of death, the Japanese usually – but not always –use *yon* for four and *nana* for seven. There are more substitutions among higher numbers. Do not laugh, Westerners are often just as nervous about the number thirteen.

PART 2 – GRAMMAR

Chapter 2-1
Grammar Model

WIKIPEDIA DEFINES GRAMMAR AS "the set of structural rules governing the composition of clauses, phrases, and words in a natural language". Unlike every other major language, the Japanese language evolved with almost no outside influence. As a result, it is unique in its structure. More importantly, where most major languages have a hodgepodge of rules due to their evolution from several different sources, Japanese grammar is for the most part internally consistent and logical. It is our purpose to present the rules in an orderly way that will help the reader see the logical structure of the language.

The Japanese sentence has:

No plurals - *sensei* can refer to one or many teachers.

No articles- Japanese does not use the equivalent of 'a,' 'an,' 'the,' *etc.*

No capital letters – except when writing in *Romaji. kana* and *kanji* have no upper/lower case

No gender – *sensei* can refer to a male or female teacher.

Few spaces – words are usually not separated by spaces.

Topics - a grammatical concept unique to the Japanese language.

Particles – that are also unique and indispensable to the Japanese language.

Verbs – always at the end of the sentence are. Otherwise, the order of elements of a sentence is generally undefined - the speaker may arrange them in any order.

Conjugation does not exist in Japanese. Almost every text promotes conjugation. It is very misleading. Instead of changing the verb, the verb modifies keys that define the tense, polarity, formality, and mode of the sentence.

Levels of speech – ranging from street talk to imperial. The two prominent levels are known by various names – we will call them informal and formal.

Reversed - the order of things is often opposite to Western thinking. For instance, what are <u>pre</u>positions in English are <u>post</u>positions in Japanese. Reversal is found throughout the culture: a person's name is family first, then given name, a book has the spine on the right, opening from what Westerners consider the back. Even the 911 emergency phone number used in the U.S. is 119 in Japan.

Do not try to apply English language rules to Japanese - you will only get confused. Unlike European languages that are similar in many ways to English, Japanese is very different. Treat it as an all-new subject. If you ever studied a computer programming language, you did not try to compare its structure and logic with English. Approach Japanese the same way.

That is not to say that learning Japanese language is easy. Although the grammar is nicely structured, the written language – with three alphabets and a couple of thousand *kanji* characters to memorize - and the counting system that is a bit crazy, can make Japanese difficult to master.

The American Foreign Service Institute is a United States government organization that prepares ambassadors and staff for foreign assignments. It teaches all the major languages and has ranked them according to the difficulty for English speakers. French, Spanish, and other European languages are the easiest, requiring 24 to 30 weeks to learn. The most difficult are Arabic, Chinese, Korean, and Japanese – requiring almost two years of study. This is not because Japanese grammar is difficult – most of the time is required for learning to read and write in unfamiliar styles. And to master the numbers - one uses different words for days of the month, people count, and more. The grammar is, in fact, the easy part.

Do not panic! This book is intended to show you that Japanese grammar is readily understood. Most textbooks and teachers present the Japanese language as sets of rules that seem disconnected. Yet there is a structure which, when recognized, logically connects those bits and pieces. Their objective is to encourage you by helping you to converse in Japanese as soon as possible and feel that you are learning. My objective is to give you a solid framework to put those rules together to understand what you are doing.

Why a Model?

Rather than listing dozens of rules, I have chosen to create a model of Japanese grammar. The Merriam Webster Dictionary defines a model as "a description or analogy used to help visualize something that cannot be directly observed".

Japanese lends itself readily to this means of presentation.

A Model of Japanese Grammar

There are many forms a model can take. The model presented here begins with the basic building blocks – words – and works its way to sentences. It makes visible the logical structure of the language and provides the user with a framework to extend his or her knowledge of the language.

This model is in four parts: words, phrases, elements, and sentences.

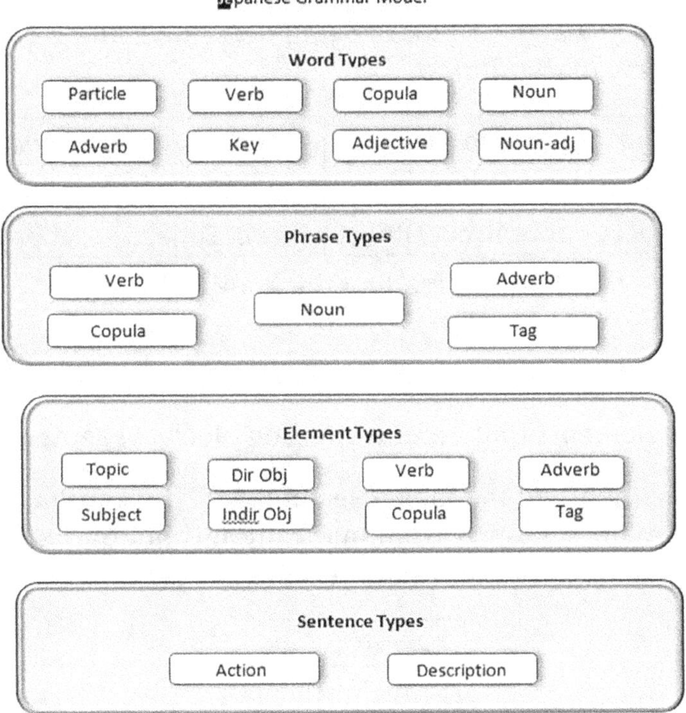

Sentences

There are two types of sentences: action, and description.

<u>*Action sentences*</u> describe an action of the subject, including what is used and who or with what it is used. An action sentence may contain any of the elements. As a minimum, it must have a subject that performs the action, and a verb that describes the action.

Aya san	wa	(watashi)	(ga)	hon	o	yonde	shi	mashita	ka
As for Aya		(Aya)		book		read	do	previously	?
Topic		Subject		Indirect Object		Verb			Tag

<u>*Description sentences*</u> describe some property of the subject. The property may be a characteristic, a state of existence, or a state of activity. A description sentence must have a subject that is being described, and a copula phrase to describe a property of the subject.

Miyuki sab	ga	Kiho san	ni	hon	o	yonde	aru
Miyuki		Kiho	to	book from		reading	is
Subject		Indirect Object	Direct Object			Copula	

Miyuki is reading the book to Kiho

Elements

There are eight elements that are the building blocks of sentences:

<u>*Topic element*</u> is unique to the Japanese language. It is optional. It defines the topic of the following sentence. Grammatically, it is not part of the sentence; it is an introduction to it, relating what the sentence is about.

watashi	wa
As for me	
Topic	

Subject element contains the subject of a sentence. It is mandatory but is often not included in the sentence, in which case, it is a virtual subject, assumed to be understood by the listener/reader. It is often the same as the topic.

watashi	ga
I	
Subject	

Direct object element tells what the action used, and

hon	o
Book	
Dir Obj	

Indirect object element tells who or what received the action

Nobuo san	ni
Nobuo	
Indir Obj	

Adverb element provides additional information about the action described by the verb.

Hiroshima	e
Hiroshima	to
Adverb	

Verb element defines the action in an action sentence,

yonde	shi	mashita
read	do	previously
Verb		

Copula element defines a property of the subject in a description sentence.

midori	desu
green	is
Copula	

Tag element provides additional information about the sentence, such as the fact that it is a question, or that it connects to another sentence, or that the speaker has some doubt, enthusiasm, or other feeling about the sentence.

ka	*demo*	*ne*
?	But	I think

Phrases

There are five phrase types. Phrases consist of a word and its modifiers. Each is used as an element of the appropriate type.

Verb phrases contain keys and a verb to define mode and action. The keys define the form (case and mode) of the action. The verb identifies the action.

The process of formation is often (incorrectly) called conjugation. Verb phrases are used as verb elements in sentences.

yonde	*shi*	*mashita*
read	do	previously
Verb		

Copula phrases contain a noun or adjective to define the properties of a subject and a copula. The property may be an attribute, state of existence, or state of activity. Copula phrases are used as copula elements.

yonde	*aru*
reading	is
Copula	

Noun phrases contain a noun and modifiers. They are used as topic, subject, direct and indirect object elements. Noun phrases use adjective phrases to modify the noun. The Japanese language does not allow modifiers to follow the item modified, so it cannot have clauses that follow the noun (*e.g.*, "Aya, who lives in Ōmori"). A preceding adjective phrase must be used ("lives in Ōmori Aya") to provide that information.

hon	*o*
book	
Noun	

<u>Adverb phrases</u> contain information to modify a verb or copula phrase They often do not contain an adverb *e.g.,* "at eight o'clock" is an adverb phrase with no adverb.

hashiku	*Nagasaki*	*e*
Quickly	Nagasaki	to
Adverb	Adverb	

<u>Tag phrases</u> contain one or more particles that follow the sentence and indicate whether it is a question, or is linked to another sentence, or to indicate a mood for the sentence.

ka
?
Tag

Words

There are eight Japanese word types used in making phrases.

<u>Particles</u> are a unique feature of the Japanese language. Most are a single *hiragana* character. Their main purpose is to define the content of noun and adverb phrases.

<u>*Noun*</u>	<u>*ga*</u>
<u>*Noun Phrase*</u>	

<u>Adverbs</u> arc words that modify a verb phrase.

hashuku
quickly

<u>Verbs</u> describe actions. Verbs have a body and a single *hiragana* character tail. There are two irregular verbs (verbs that do not behave the same as the others). The rest are divided into two groups. Excepting for the two irregulars, the body never changes. The basic form of a verb is the dictionary (non-past tense positive informal) form.

yoru
read

Copulas are special verbs or adjectives that define some property of a subject.

aru
is

Adjectives can be used without the copula _da_ in informal non-past sentences. The tail of all adjectives is always _i._

chisai
Small is

Noun-adjs are a class of nouns that can serve as adjectives to modify other nouns. _na_ is required between the Noun-adj <u>and</u> the noun being modified.

genki	genki na
health	healthy
Noun	Adjective

Keys are special words that define the form (tense, mode, _etc._) of a sentence. Verbs, copulas, and _i_-adjectives have bodies that never change, and a tail that can change. Formation (that many incorrectly call conjugation) is achieved by changing the tail and appending key words.

mashita
was

Nouns are names of real or abstract things, including people.

Body and Tail

Except for the two irregular verbs, the body of a word never changes. The tail can change according to the use.

Since Japanese writing has no spaces, the body, tail, and keys of a verb phrase are run together, and it appears that the verb is changing. It is not. The only thing that changes is the tail. Keys are added.

Word Type	Changes?	
	Body	Tail
Particle	no	n/a
Adverb	no	n/a
Verb	no*	yes
Key	no	yes
Copula	no	yes
Adjective	no	yes
Noun-adj	no	n/a
Adverb	no	n/a

* except Group 3 irregulars

Words can be changed from one type to another.

This is a quick overview. In the remainder of this text, each component of the model is discussed. The order is reversed, starting with words, then phrases, elements, and sentences.

Chapter 2.2
DEFINITIONS

THE JAPANESE LANGUAGE DIFFERS FROM ENGLISH IN MANY WAYS. It is necessary to use different words to describe some features. Also, linguists have their own vocabulary that is not necessarily understood by us lay people. For instance, past perfect progressive means actions that were in progress shortly before or up to a past time. Odds are this was not obvious to you. So here I call this 'past ongoing.' I have changed the names of several other items from the normally taught terms.

General Rules

First let us list a few general rules.

The verb element is always the last element of the sentence or adjective phrase. (tag elements are not considered part of the sentence and do come after the verb element).

The modifiers of a word always precede the word. English clauses like "who fell down" or "that ran with me" are implemented as adjective phrases so that they precede the noun they are modifying.

All verbs in a sentence, excepting those in the main (last) verb element, must be in the informal case.

Modify

We frequently say some word modifies another. By that, we mean it provides more information. For instance, an adverb may modify a verb, such as 'quickly ran;' 'quickly' provides more information about the verb 'ran.' Similarly, an adjective may modify a noun, such as 'big tree.' In either case, in Japanese the modifiers must precede the modified word.

Body and Tail

All words have bodies that never change. Verbs, copulas, s, and adjectives have tails that change according to their use.

Tail Category

Group 1 verb tails are categorized according to form.

Form Category	Tail Category
Negative	a
Formal	i
Informal	u
Command & Conditional	e
Volitional	o

For Group 1 verbs, different forms cause only the vowel of the tail to change. For instance, *mu* can change to *ma, mi, me,* or *mo.*

Adjective

Adjectives are usually called *i* adjectives. They are the true adjective in the Japanese language. In informal descriptive sentences, they can serve as the complete copula phrase; no *da* is required.

chīsai
Small is
Copula

Noun-adj

Noun-adjs are usually called *na* adjectives. They are only adjectives when *na* is appended. Otherwise, they are nouns. It is better to emphasize the noun aspect and observe that it can also be used as an adjective, by calling it a noun-adj.

Tense

Tense is the expression of when an event occurred. There are two tense values in the Japanese language: past, and non-past.

<u>Past tense</u> is used for events that have completed by the time of the statement.

Non-past tense applies to events that have not completed (present)including those that have not even started (future).

Future tense does not exist. Stating a time with a non-past tense verb form establishes a future event. Note that the verb form for the present and future is the same in the following examples.

Examples

Past	**Present**	**Future**
kinō **nomi mashitta**	_kyo **nomi masu**_	_ashita **nomi masu**_
yesterday I drink did	today I drink	tomorrow I drink

Polarity – is the expression of a positive or negative statement. Negative is not an action; it is a state of being. Therefore, it is represented by an adjective instead of a verb.

Examples

Positive	I sleep	Is an Action	Uses a Verb
Negative	I do not sleep	Is a State of being	Uses an Adjective

Formality - is the degree of respect in speaking. It is expressed in the verb phrase, and in the choice of some words. In this text, we recognize two levels of formality: informal, and formal. These are often called by other names. There is no equivalent in English.

Informal speech is used among close friends, and by superiors speaking to lower-ranked persons.

Formal speech is used by persons speaking to anyone who is not clearly lower ranked.

Case is the combination of tense, polarity, and formality. There are eight cases:

Informal Non-past Positive	Formal Non-past Positive
Informal Past Positive	Formal Past Positive
Informal Non-past Negative	Formal Non-past Negative
Informal Past Negative	Formal Past Negative

Mode

is the type of sentence: command, suggestion, desire, ability, *etc.* The mode of a sentence is expressed in the verb phrase.

There are many modes – we have chosen the most common modes for illustration. Also, we include the *te* form as a mode. While not a mode, it is formed in the same manner.

Able-to expresses something that can be done by the subject. It is usually called potential mode.

Cause-Let - expresses something the subject causes or allows another to n the negative, prevents someone from doing. It is usually called causative.

Command - Avoid using this mode. It is used mostly by police or parents with their children, and on public road signs (*e.g.,* Stop). It should only be used for emergencies where, for instance, there is no time for being polite. It is usually called imperativ*e*.

Let's - This mode changes a statement into a suggestion. Usually interpreted as "Let's .. ". It is often simply called the *mashyo* mode. It expresses an invitation or suggestion for action, such as "Let's eat," or "Let's see a movie". It is usually called volitional or presumptive mode.

Want - often simply called the *tai* or desire form, expresses the subject's appeal to the speaker. The subject inspires a desire I the speaker. It is usually called desire or *tai* form.,

If-Then - is a condition of the form "if X is true, then Y is true" (*e.g.,* If it rains, I will go inside). It is usually called the *ba* or hypothetical form

If-Once, a conditional of the form "if X is true, then Y is true. "It differs from If-Then in that it can be used for both hypothetical (*e.g.,* if I fail the test, I will cry) and actual (*e.g.,* if I can afford it, I will go to America) conditionals.

If-Context, a conditional of the form "if X is true, Y is true". The statement is used in response to a context in the conversation, *e.g*".I am going to eat now" (the context) –"If you are going to eat now, I will go to eat also" (the response). Usually called the *tara* form, it always follows a past tense verb, one that ends with *ta*, so it could be called the *ra* form.

If-Always, a conditional of the form "if X is true, then Y is always true". This links sentences with 'and' e.g., "it is March <u>and</u> cherry trees are blossoming".

te form – is not strictly a mode, but since it is implemented in the same process, is included here. The *te* form's primary function is linking verbs or adjectives. It has many applications in this role.

Form

is the name for the case and mode of a verb phrase. Thus, the form of a sentence might be (past positive formal) (want) – expressing an earlier desire.

Case	Modes	
	Command	Want
Tense	Able-to	If-then
Polarity	Cause-Let	If-context
Formality	Let's	If-always
	Receiving	If-once

Conjugation

Conjugation is altering a verb according to tense, plurality, *etc.* Japanese do not alter words. Japanese text has no spaces between words. As a result, people tend to view certain combinations as single words. For instance, *tabe masu* means eat, and *tabe mashita* means eat did, or ate. Many think these are single words - *tabemasu* and *tabemashita* and *tabemashita and* call the process pf changing conjugation. But the verb did not change.

The verb is a modifier for the key(s). *tabe mashita* is past tense (*mashita*) modified by eat (*tabe).* It is incorrect to call the process conjugation. There is no conjugation in Japanese. I choose to call the process formation: forming the verb and keys of a verb phrase.

Formation

In this model, formation means the process of implementing the form of a verb phrase

Tail

Verbs and adjectives have a tail. The tail is a single *hiragana* character at the end of the word.

<u>Examples</u>

Verb	Dictionary Form	Tail		Adjective	Dictionary Form	Tail
hana	*hanasu*	*su*		*chīsa*	*chīsa*	*i*
tabe	*taberu*	*ru*		*atsui*	*atsu*	*i*
no	*nomu*	*mu*		*sukanai*	*sukana*	*i*
ka	*kau*	*u*		*koshii*	*koshi*	*i*

Except for the two irregular verbs, the verb <u>never</u> changes. The tail changes according to the form. Similarly, the adjective never changes. The tail can change.

Tag

Sentences are often followed by one or more particles. It is not always part of the grammatical sentence, but it provides the listener extra information. The question tag acts like a question mark and makes the sentence into a question. The mood tag expresses something about the sentence, while the connector connects the sentence to another sentence, and a condition tag connects to another sentence to express an" if-then" type of statement.

<u>Question Tag</u>

Question (k*a*) converts the sentence to a question.

<u>Mood Tags</u>

Surprise (*no*) expresses reconfirmation or surprise

Confirm (*ne*) requests confirmation or agreement. Often translated as "don't you agree?"

Information (*yo*) providing new information, or like an exclamation mark, also for commands and invitations

Emphasis (*zo*) often used in a shout, a call, or a yell, used only by men

Admire (*na*) expresses a personal emotion or desire **Prohibition** (*na*) expresses prohibition when placed after **Uncertain** (*kana*) expresses uncertainty

Thought (*wa*) declares a personal thought

Attention (*sa*) used to draw attention with a pause

Connector

And (*society*) – connects to another sentence.

Conditions

If-Then (*ba*) – general-purpose if A then B

If -Once (*ra*) – if A happened, then B happened

If -Response (*nara*) – used in response to a question.

If -Always (*to*) – if A occurs the B always occurs.

Chapter 2-3
WORD TYPES

WORDS ARE THE BASIS OF ALL LANGUAGES. Japanese has the usual noun, verb, copula, and adverb. Japanese also has a noun type that can also be an adjective and an adjective type that can also include a copula. Particles and keys are unique to the language. Particles are used primarily to identify the type of content contained in noun phrases and as conjunctions. Keys are used in verb phrases to express he mode of a sentence.

Nomenclature

I take the liberty of changing the names of some word types:

>   auxiliary -> key
>   *i* adjective -> adjective
>   *na* adjective -> noun-adj

I do this to make it easier to understand these items.

Auxiliaries come at the end of the sentence, after the sentence's main verb. Traditionally, it is said that they help the verb. But modifiers precede the modified word. The verb is modifying the key.

<u>Example</u>

tabe	*rare*	*masen*
eat	able to	not
verb	key	key

The important part is 'not.' Not what? Not able. Not able to what? Not able to eat. The verb is helping the keys, not the other way around. I think calling them helpers or auxiliaries is misleading. I admit that key is an odd choice, but I could find no better name. It is the key to the mode of the sentence – in this case, 'not able.'

What is usually called a *na* adjective is a special noun. It is only an adjective when followed by a *na* particle. Other nouns can become adjectives using *no*, but they are not called *no* adjectives.

<u>Example</u>

yūnē   *yūnē na hito*
Fame   Famous person
Noun   Adjective

To call *yūnē* an adjective is misleading. It is a noun that can be made into an adjective. I call it a noun-adj.

The only true Japanese adjective is what is normally called the *i* adjective.

<u>Example</u>

chīsai hon
Small book

There is no need to distinguish this adjective from noun-adjs. It is an adjective and I call it that.

Tail

Verbs, copulas, and adjectives have a tail that is a single *hiragana* character. The tail connects the word to the following word. Unlike most other languages words are not changed (except for two irregular verbs) for tense, *etc.* Instead, keys are used to relate the case and mode. The verb modifies the keys.

<u>Examples</u>

Type	**Example**	**Word**	**Tail**
Group 1 Verb	*kiku*	*ki*	*ku*
Group2 Verb	*ageru*	*age*	*ru*
Group 3 Verb	*kuru*	*ku*	*ru*
Adjective	*chīsai*	*chīsa*	*i*

tabe	*mashita*
eat Verb	*did* Key
ate Verb Phrase	

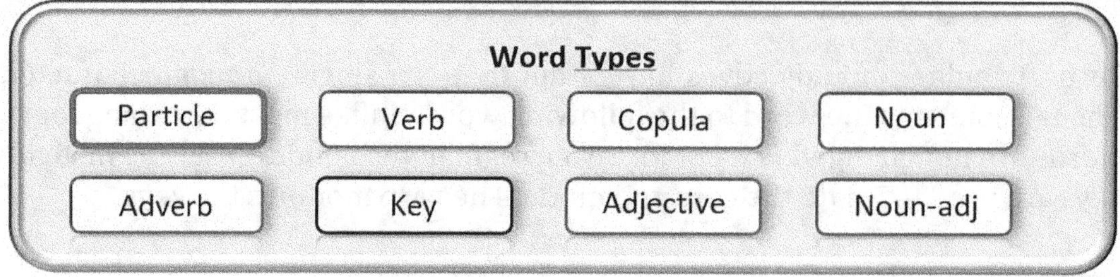

Particle

Particles are unique to the Japanese language. And they are critical. Appearing at the end of phrases, they identify the type of information contained in the phrase. Seemingly related in many ways to English prepositions, some particles serve to identify phrases relating to when or where the action is taking place. Others identify the role of phrases in a sentence, such as subject, direct object, *etc.* And others identify phrases as containing amounts and more. They occur at the end of noun and adverb phrases to identify their content and are also used as sentence endings. Without particles, the Japanese language does not work.

Some particles are used to indicate the grammatic role of a noun phrase – topic, subject, indirect or direct object. Others are used in adverb phrases.

Particles are written in *hiragana* and are usually just one character but can be longer. Some particles have more than one meaning, made clear by the context. There are many particles; some are frequently used; some are quite rare.

(Mis)pronunciation of some particles

The topic particle *wa* is written as *ha* (は), the direct object particle *o* is written as *wo* (を), and a particle for direction *(e)* is written as *he* (へ). These are holdovers from ancient days – the pronunciation changed over time, but the writing did not. We portray them as they are pronounced: *wa*, o, and *e*, respectively.

Translation of Particles

Many particles have more of a theme than a simple meaning. For instance, *ni* marks a destination or end point in a broad sense, including a physical destination or the recipient of the action of the verb in a sentence, *i.e.,* the indirect object of the verb. Although in the following, a translation is shown for each particle, it is better to think it is telling what the preceding noun is about. For instance, in the following phrase *ni* is shown to mean 'at'.

<u>Example</u>

ku ji	*ni*
9 o'clock	at

Better to think it means "the preceding (*ku ji*) is the location in time of the action". Please keep this in mind as you read the examples below.

Common Particles

<u>wa</u>–The primary function of *wa* is to identify the topic of the sentence.

<u>Example</u>

Keiko san	**wa**
Keiko san	
Topic	

<u>wa</u> is an inclusive particle. For instance, *watashi wa* means 'I' and implies "I, among others".

wa is also used in comparisons.

<u>Example</u>

gohan	**wa**	*tabe*	*mashita*		*ga*		*niku*	**wa**	*tabe*	*masen*	*deshita.*
Rice		eat	did		but		meat		eat	not	did
DirObj		Verb			Tag		DirObj		Verb		

One might expect *o* to be used to mark the direct object, but for comparisons, *wa* is preferred.

mo is an inclusive particle that means part of a set. A set is a group of like things. For instance, one might say "George is also a student in my class". George is being identified as a member of the "students in the class" set. *mo* is usually described as meaning 'also' or 'too' and has many related purposes. It may be used as an alternate to *wa* as a topic marker, to mean 'also.'

Related uses include "as well as," "and," "in addition," "a number of times," "always," "as much as," and defining an approximate upper limit.

Also, too

Better described as "in the set," *i.e.,* defines the word as being in a set of things.

Examples

waatashi	*mo*
I also	

I also (I am a member of the set of people)

america-jin	*mo*	*chuugokujin*	*mo*
American	also	Chinese	also

American and Chinese
American and Chinese are in the set of nationalities

All of, as much as

Example

daigakusei	*mo*	*shitte*	*i*	*masu*
students	all	know	state	is

Knows all students (knows the set of students)

Up to (amount)

Example

san ju nichi	*mo*
30 days	up to

Up to 30 days (the set has 30 days)

<u>*mo combined with other particles.*</u>

demo – **even if** (with *te* form verb)

Example

yuki	*ga*	*futte*	*demo,*
snow		fall	even if

Even if snowfalls

Falling snow is in the set of possible events.

nanimo – **nothing** (with negative verb phrase) - no item in set

Example

nanimo	*shira*	*nai*
nothing	know	not

Knows nothing (knows nothing is the set)

dokomo – **everywhere (all places in set)**

Example

dokomo	*ii*	*desu*
everywhere	good	is

Everywhere is good (every place in the set of places is good)

daremo - **anyone (any person in set)**

Example

daremo	*nome*	*ru*
Anyone	drink	can

Anyone can drink (any person in set can drink)

daremo - **No-one** (with negative verb) (no one in set)

Example

dare mo	*noma*	*nai*
Everyone	drink	not

No one drinks (all people in set do not drink)

ga Its primary function is identifying a noun phrase as the sentence subject.

In addition, it is used to connect two sentences with 'but' or 'although.'

<u>Example</u>

watashi	*ga*	*bīru*	*o*	*nomi*	*mashita*		***ga***
I		beer		drink	did		but

sake	*wa*	*nomi*	*masen*	*deshita*
sake		drink	not	did

I drank beer but did not drink sake.

---

o - marks the direct object of the verb.

The object is what is being used to accomplish the verb action.

<u>Example</u>

hana	*o*	*age*	*mashita*
flower		give	did
Dir Obj		Verb	

Flower gave

---

ni identifies the target of action. It can be the time or frequency, or a location.

<u>Examples</u>

ku ji	***ni***
9 o'clock at	

rittoru	***ni***	*20 kiromētoru*
liter per		kilometer

wei	***ni***
top on	

ni also identifies the indirect object of the verb, which is the target of the action.

<u>Example</u>

Keiko san	***ni***	*hana*	*o*	*age*	*mashita*
Keiko	to	flower		give	did
Indir Obj		Dir Obj		Verb	

flower gave to Keiko

_e_ - a direction or destination

Example

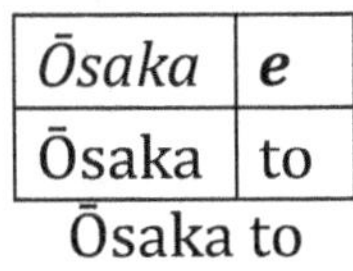

or the goal of movement is Ōsaka

Both _ni_ and _e can_ define a destination or direction. They are well described as defining the goal of movement. You can say _gakkō ni iku_ or _gakkō e iku_ (I am going to school) and _gakkō ni iru_ (I am at school), but you cannot say _gakkō e iru_ , because _e_ implies motion, and being at school is no a motion.

_no_ – is a modifier; it converts a verb into a noun and noun into an adjective.

Many texts say that _no_ is a possessive - an equivalent to 's, and that is often true, as in _Ikuyo no uchi_ - "Ikuyo's house". But _ishi no uchi_ is not "stone's house". It is "house of stone". It is better to think of _no_ as 'of' (with Japanese usual reversal of order): "house of Ikuyo" and "house of stone".

It is best to think of _no_ as converting a noun to an adjective. _Ikuyo no uchi_ becomes "Ikuyo(s) house," and _ishi no uchi_ becomes "stone house".

_no_ also converts a verb to an adjective. _hachiru no kodomo_ is "running child.

Examples

Ikuyo	_**no**_	_uchi_		_ishi_	_**no**_	_uchi_		_hachiru_	_**no**_	_kodomo_
Ikuyo('s)		house		stone		house		running		child

_no_ is also used to specify a location; Again, it is an adjective. If the verb defines an action, you must use _de_ instead of _no_.

Example

hako	_**no**_	_naka_	_ni_
box ('s)		inside	at

One does not say "inside the box," instead on says "at the box's inside". The inside, top, side, _etc._ are properties of the box.

A sentence may have many *nos* chained.

<u>Example</u>

watashi	*no*	*tomodachi*	*no*	*aka*	*no*	*Nihon*	*no*	*kuruma*
my		friend's		red		Japanese		car

no can also convert a noun to a pronoun. Better to think of the pronoun as an adjective, which is what *no* is all about.

<u>Example</u>

watachi no	*kare no*	*dare no*
my	his	who's

<u>de</u> - is a versatile particle that adds information about how the verb acts. It can tell

> where the action takes place,
> what is used to achieve the action,
> what components are used to accomplish the action,
> what the categories of components are,
> relate quantities and measurements associated with the action,
> identify groups of people involved in the action, and
> establish time limits for the action.

<u>Examples</u>

Location of the action

Shinagawa	*de*	*tabe*	*mashita*
Shinigawa	in	eat	did

koen	*de*	*aruki*	*mashita*
Park in		walk	did

intanetto	*de*	*kotae ga*	*mitsukari*	*mashita*
internet	on	answer	find	did

Do not confuse *de* with *ni*. *de* marks the location of some action, while *ni* marks where something exists.

Tools used to achieve action

jitensha	*de*	koen	e	iki	mashita
bicycle	**by**	park	to	go	did

sakana	to	gohan	*de*	sushi o	tsukuru
(with) fish	and	rice		sushi	make

Components used to accomplish the action

tsukue	wa	ki	*de*	dekite	i masu
desk		wood	**of**	make	do

Define a category

kuruma	de	sukina	no	wa	Subaru	desu
cars	of all	favorite			Subaru	is

Quantities and measurements associated with the action

ringo	wa	ju ko	*de*	hyaku	en	desu
apples		ten		100	yen	are

Apples are 10 for 100 yen

kuruma	wa	1 rittotu	*de*	23 kiro	shutoku	shi	masu
car		one liter	per	23 kilometers	obtain		does

Car 23 kilometers per liter gets

Groups of people involved in the action

san	hito	*de*	benkyo	Shi	masu
three	people		study		do

Three people study

Set time limits for the action

go	fun	de	hanshi	masu
five	minutes	limit	speak	do

Speak for five minutes

de is also the *te* for of the copula *da*, which we will discover later.

<u>*to*</u> – and

<u>Example</u>

Mitsuyoshi san	*to*	*Kiho san*
Mitsuyoshi	and	Kiho

Mitsuyoshi and Kiho

<u>*dake*</u> – *just, only,* a limit on things or amounts.

<u>Example</u>

josei	*dake*
women	only

For women only

<u>*ka*</u> – or

<u>Example</u>

ringo	*ka*	*orenji*
Apple	or	Orange

Apple or orange

<u>*kan*</u> - a duration of time

<u>Example</u>

san ji	*kan*
three hours	duration

Three hours long

<u>*kara*</u> - a starting point in time or place (origin)

<u>Example</u>

Kyuahu	*kara*
Kyushu	From

From Kyushu

8:15	*Kara*
8:15 o'clock	from

Starting at 8:15

made - a limit on time (end), space (destination), or quantity

<u>Example</u>

Hokkaido	*made*
Hokkaido	To (destination)

9:00	*made*
9 o'clock	To (end time)

5 kilograms	*made*
5 kg	To (limit)

nado - the end of a partial list of multiple items (*etc.*)

ya - a connection of items in a partial list

<u>Example</u>

A	*ya*	B	*ya*	C	*nado*
A	and	B	and	C,	*etc.*

A, B, and C, *etc.*

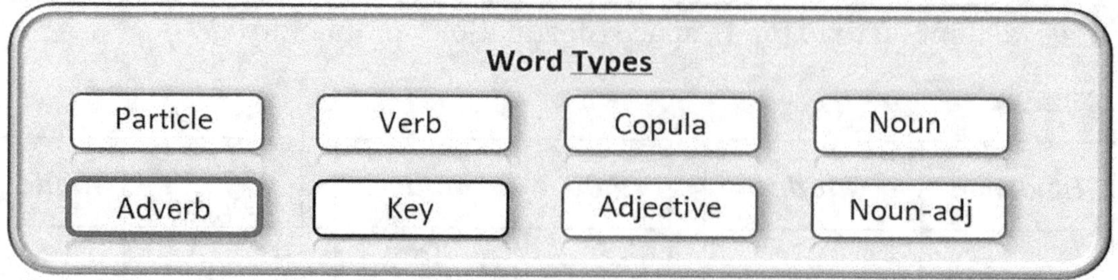

Adverb

In the English phrase "walked quickly," 'quickly' is an adverb modifying the verb 'walk.' Japanese also has adverbs. They are used to modify verbs, nouns, adjectives, and other adverbs. They can tell how, when, why, or where an action happens. They can also provide information about manner, frequency, duration, or method. There are 'pure' adverbs and others converted from other word types. Here is a sampling of adverbs.

sukkari	completely	*tokodoki*	sometimes
sukoshi	a little	*yoku*	often
sukunai	a few	*yukkuri*	slowly
tabun	perhaps	*zenzen*	completely
taihen	very	*mainichi*	everyday
taitei	usually	*mata*	again
takusan	a lot	*motto*	more
tamani	rarely	*nanimo*	not at all

Adverbs from Adjectives

Adjectives can be converted to adverbs. To make an adverb from an adjective, replace the tail (*i*) with *ku*.

<u>Examples</u>

Adjective	**Adverb**
(busy) *isogashii*	*isogashiku* (busily)
(cheap*) yasui*	*yasuku* (cheaply*)*
(good*) yoi*	*yoku* (well*)*
(happy*) ureshii*	*ureshiku* (happily*)*
(quick*) hayai*	*hayaku* (quickly)

Adverbs from Noun-adjs

Adverbs can also be converted from noun-adjs. To make an adverb from a noun-adj, just add the particle *ni.*

<u>Examples</u>

Noun-Adj	**Adverb**
(clean) *kirei*	*kirei ni* (cleanly)
(easy) *kantan*	*kantan ni* (easily)
(magnificent) *karei*	<u>*karei ni* (magnificently)</u>
(quiet) *shizuka*	*shizuka ni* (quietly)
(simple) *kantan*	*kantan ni* (simply)
(skillful) *jōzu*	*jōzu ni* (skillfully)

Some adverbs will seem strange to non-Japanese. For instance, a long time can be said as *nagaku*, which translates (sort of) to long time:

<u>Example</u>

koko	*ni*	*nagaku*	*sunde*	*i*	*mashita*
here	at	longly	live	be	did

Lived here a long time

<u>*Changes*</u>

Ad adverb followed by *suru* (do) means a willful change, while an adverb followed by *naru* (begin) means a natural change.

<u>Examples</u>

yoju	*suru*
goodly	do

Make better

yoku	*naru*
goodly	become

Become better

Placement of adverbs

When an adverb modifies a noun, an adjective, or another adverb, it must be placed immediately before it.

Examples

taihen akai   _taitei yoku_
Very red   Usually often

However, when an adverb modifies a verb, it may be placed anywhere before the verb.

Examples

yoku _Onodera san ga ofisu ni itte imasu_
Onodera san ga **yoku** ofisu ni itte imasu
Onodera san ga ofisu ni **yoku** itte imasu
Onodera office to **often** go does

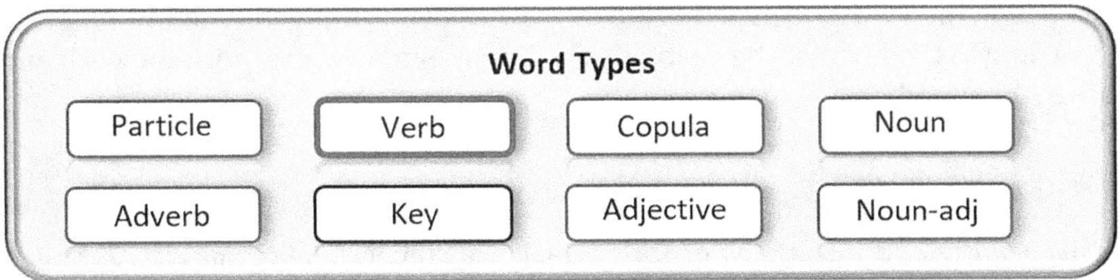

Verb

Verbs are where the action is.

Dictionary Form

English dictionaries order verbs alphabetically by the infinitive form, *e.g.,* 'to hear.' The Japanese verbs are ordered by the informal non-past positive form. Accordingly, it is called the Dictionary Form.

Tail

Verbs have a tail that is a single *hiragana* character at the end of the verb. Examples

Verb*	Verb	Tail
tanomu	*tano*	*mu*
taberu	*tabe*	*ru*
suru	*su*	*ru*

*Dictionary Form

The dictionary form for every verb has a tail from the *u* row (or column, depending on the orientation) of the *hiragana* table (below). Thus, every dictionary form verb ends with the u sound: *u, ku, gu, su, tsu, nu, bu, mu,* or *ru.* There are other characters in that row, but they are not used by any verb.

Partial *hiragana* Table

a	ka	ga	sa	ta	na	ba	ma	ra
i	*ki*	*gi*	*shi*	*chi*	*ni*	*bi*	*mi*	*ri*
u	*ku*	*gu*	*su*	*tsu*	*nu*	*bu*	*mu*	*ru*
e	*ke*	*ge*	*se*	*te*	*ne*	*be*	*me*	*re*
o	*ko*	*go*	*so*	*to*	*no*	*bo*	*mo*	*ro*

Except for the two irregular verbs, the verb never changes. The tail changes according to the form of the verb phrase. For irregular verbs, both the verb and tail are changed.

Verb Groups

Verbs are divided into three groups which we cleverly call groups 1, 2, and 3. The formation process is dependent on the group. Since group 1 is 'all other,' we will leave it to last and begin with group 3.

<u>Group 3</u> contains the irregular verbs. Unlike English, where it seems every other verb has an irregular conjugation (*e.g.*, see-saw, go-went, hear-heard), there are only two in common Japanese - *kuru* (come) and *suru* (do).

<u>Group 2</u> verbs are also known as *ichidan* verbs because the dictionary form tail has only one (*ichi*) value - the dictionary form tail of all Group 2 verbs is *ru:* specifically, *eru* or *iru* when written in *Romaji.* However, just to keep you on your toes, not all verbs with the tail *ru* are in Group 2. There is no simple rule for determining which verbs end withe *eru* or *iru* but belong in Group 1. It usually has to do with the *kanji* in the word.

<u>Examples</u>

<u>Group 2</u>		<u>Group 1</u>	
*tabe**ru***	eat	*kae**ru***	return home
*mi**ru***	see	*shime**ru***	be damp

<u>Group 1</u> is also called *godan* for the five (*go*) possible values a tail might have. It consists of all verbs that are not in Groups 2 or 3, *i.e.*, do not have *ru* as the tail (with exceptions, see above) and are not the irregular verbs *kuru* or *suru*.

<u>Examples</u>

*a**u***	meet	*shi**nu***	die
*ki**ku***	hear	*to**bu***	fly
*kase**gu***	earn	*su**mu***	reside
*ta**su***	stand	*u**ru***	sell
*hana**tsu***	set free		

A piece of trivia: *shinu* (die) is the only verb whose dictionary form has the tail *nu*

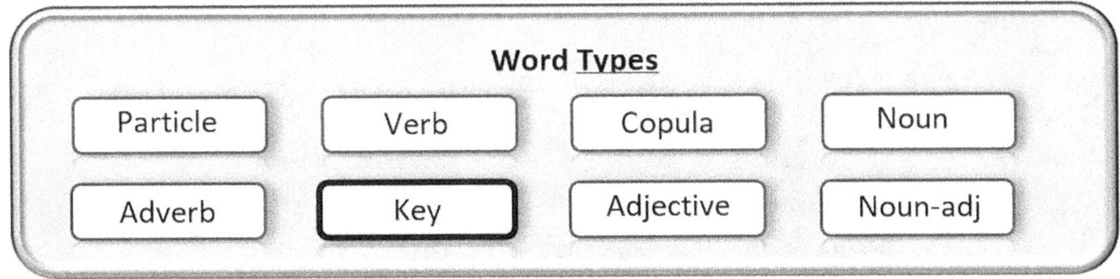

Key

Usually called auxiliary verbs, keys are special verbs and adjectives. They can only be used in verb and copula phrases; they cannot be used as independent verbs or adjectives. Changing the form of a verb phrase is accomplished by changing the tail of the verb and adding the appropriate key(s). We are adding the *te* form to the mode list since it is formed by the same rules.

Case keys

Case key are words that are added to the verb to indicate the case of the sentence.

Case			Key	
Informal	Positive	Non-Past	(none)	Verb
		Past	*tta*	Verb
	Negative	Non-Past	*nai*	adjective
		Past	*nakatta*	Adjective
Formal	Positive	Non-Past	*masu*	Verb
		Past	*mashita*	Verb
	Negative	Non-Past	*masen*	Adjective
		Past	*masen deshi ta*	Adjective

Because the negative forms describe states of being instead of actions, the keys are adjectives instead of verbs and are considered in this model to be copulas.

<u>Examples</u>

tabe masu (*masu* is a verb)
Eat

tabe masen (*masen* is an adjective)
Not eat

Mode Keys

Here are the keys for the most common modes:

Mode	**Key**	**Mode**	**Key**
Able-to	*rareru*	Want	*tai*
Cause-Let	*seru*	If-Always	*to*
Command	*ro*	If-Context	*nara*
Receiving	*reru*	If-Once	*ra*
Suggestion	*yo**	If-Then	*ba*

* Formal form is *mashyo*

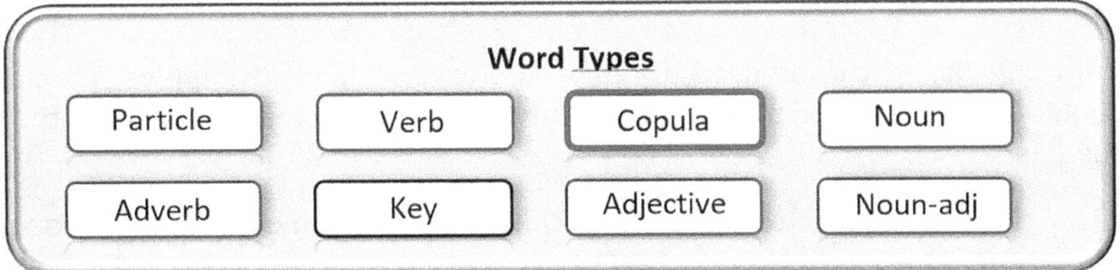

Copula

The word copula is from the Latin 'to couple.' A copula is a special form of verb that is used in descriptive sentences to couple the subject to the state of being of the subject. It may be a property, or the state of existence, or state of continuing action of the subject. There is no action associated with a copula.

The English copula is 'is' in its many forms (be, are, am, was, ..). The Japanese copulas are:

Informal	Formal	Couples	To
da	*desu*	Subject	Attribute or identity
aru	*ari masu*	Inanimate subject	State of existence
iru	*i masu*	Animate subject	State of existence
		Subject	State of continuing action

Property of the Subject

Nouns can have physical attributes such as color, weight, material, ownership, *etc.*, and they can have abstract attributes such as pretty or likable. They may also have properties that are states of being, such as existing, walking, *etc.*

<u>Examples</u>

<u>Simple attributes</u>
Color (red, white, grey, ...)
Material (wood, metal, ...)
Owner (you, me, Risa, ...)
Identity (Chinese,

<u>States of being</u>
Exists (in stock, ...)
Location (inside, in Kōbe, next to, ...)
Action (running, eating, ...)
Negative states

Existence

With English, 'is' can be used to relate existence: "There **are** apples," "It is a book". *da and desu* cannot be used here. Instead, Japanese has two other copulas:

> *iru* is used for living, animate things (animals, including the human kind) and

> *aru* for all others (trees, rocks, pencils, *etc.*).

These couple the subject to its state of existence.

Examples

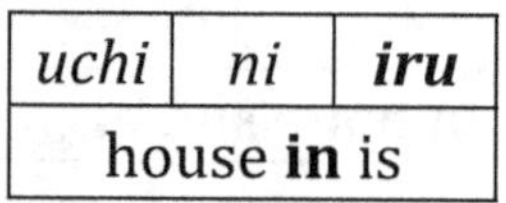

ringo	*ga*	*ari*	*masu*		*inu*	*ga*	*i*	*masu*
apples		**exist**			dog		**exists**	

Existence can relate where a thing exists.

Examples

uchi	*ni*	*iru*
house	**in** is	

(person) is in the house

shako	*no*	*naka*	*ni*	*aru*
garage's inside				**is**

(car) is inside garage

Ongoing Action

Another state of being is a continuing action. In English, 'ing' is usually added to a verb to indicate ongoing activity., "eating". In Japanese, it is achieved by using the *te* form of the verb, followed by *iru*. Since to be an ongoing action, the subject must be animated, therefore *aru* is never used.

Example

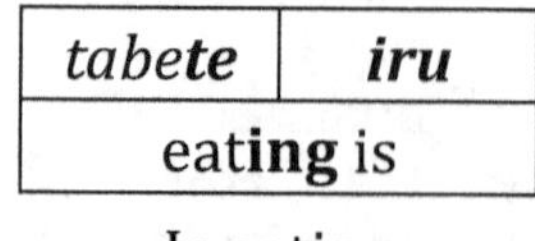

tabete	*iru*
eat**ing** is	

Is eating

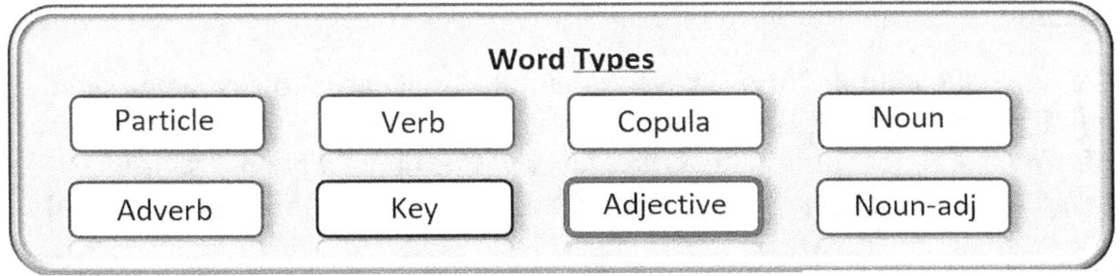

Adjective

Most texts say there are two types of adjectives: *i* adjectives and *na* adjectives. But *na* adjectives, which we will visit later, are nouns, not adjectives. They are the only adjectives are true adjectives, and we will simply call them adjectives. The *i* is unnecessary.

The tail is always the *hiragana* character *i*, as in *chiisai, ōkii, takai, etc.* But again, be warned – not every word ending with *i* is an adjective. That is usually because the written form ends with a *kanji* character. One exception – *kirei* (pretty or clean) is usually cited - even though it is written in *hiragana* as *kirei* (きれい) and ends with *i*, it is a *noun-adj* (by what authority we do not know.) Do not let the *Romaji* mislead you with words that end with an *i* sound – if it ends with *ki, shi, mi, etc.*, it does not end with the *hiragana i* and is not an adjective.

An adjective is used to modify a noun. It must immediately precede the noun.

Example

isogashii	*hito*
busy	person

Busy person

Adjective as Copula

The adjective contains the (invisible) copula *da.* That is to say, when used to define the property of the subject in an informal sentence, *da* is not required. Informal sentences simply use the adjective. To make a formal sentence, add *desu.* The presence of *desu* overrides the *da* and makes the sentence formal.

<u>Examples</u>

One can say "is red" four different ways:

<u>Informal</u>   <u>Formal</u>

aka da   akai   *aka desu   akai desu*

Is red   Is red

In the left-hand example, *aka* (red) is a noun and requires the copula *da.*

In the second column, *akai* (is red) is an *adjective*, and the unspoken copula (*da)* is not required.

In the third column, like the first, a copula is required, but now it is the formal *desu.*

In the fourth column, even though *akai* contains a copula, it is overridden by *desu* to make the sentence formal.

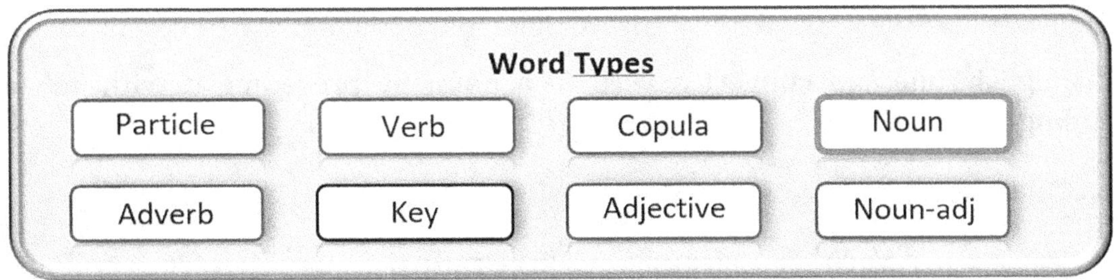

Noun

As in most languages, a noun is the name of a person, place, or thing - real or abstract. A noun may consist of several words. Japanese nouns do not have plural forms nor (as in Spanish and other languages) expression of gender.

<u>Examples</u>

<u>Sample nouns</u>

gozen go ji	5 pm
uma	Horse
John Jacob Dinkleheimer Schmidt	John Jacob Dinkleheimer Schmidt
empitsu	Pencil
Matsuoka Takumi san	Takumi Matsuoka
shisō	Thought
ku gatsu ju ichi nichi kayoubi	Tuesday, September 11
Igirisu	United Kingdom

Japanese nouns do not have a plural form. Consider these phrases

kuruma	*3-dai no kuruma*
car	Three cars

Notice that *kuruma* (car) is the same for one car and three cars. (*dai* is a counter for cars).

Nouns from verbs

In English, one can convert a verb to a noun by preceding it with 'to' or adding 'ing.'

<u>Examples</u>

Verb	Noun	Example
See	Seeing	Seeing is believing
	To see	To see is to believe

Adding *koto* or *no* to a verb changes it to a noun phrase.

<u>Examples</u>

Verb	Noun Phrase
miru (see)	*miru no* (seeing)
suru (do)	*suru no* or *suru koto* (doing)

There are times when only *no* or only *koto* should be used.

<u>Use *no* but not *koto*</u> when:
the verb is related to another's actions, such as *matsu* (wait) or *tetsudauu* (help)

<u>Examples</u>

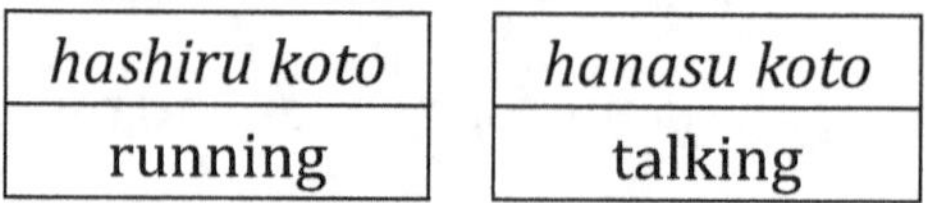

matte	iru	no
waiting		

aruku	no
walk	

<u>Use *koto* but not *no*</u> when in a descriptive sentence (using *desu*) or when the verb expresses communication or thought

<u>Examples</u>

hashiru koto
running

hanasu koto
talking

Time nouns

Time may be a clock time or a calendar time, or both. Times may represent time of an event, start time, end time, or duration. Times should be expressed as largest to smallest, *i.e.,* year, month, day, day of week, hour, minute, second.

Often, year is given in a traditional Japanese form based on the ruling emperor. The name of the era is defined by the emperor. For instance, Emperor *Akihito* was installed in 1989, making that year *Heisei* 1. 2019 began as *Heisei* 31. On May 1, 2019, Emperor *Naruhito* was enthroned, so the remainder of the year was *Reiwa* 1.

Examples

Time Nouns

1954	1954
heisei 29-nen 11 gatsh 8 nichi suiyōbi	2017, November 8, Wednesday
san ju ppun kan	30 minutes duration
ku ji 9 o'clock *saikin*	Recently
kayōbi	Tuesday
itsu	When

Location Nouns

A noun can describe a location. It may be the location of a country, city, store, an object on a table, *etc.*

Examples

Location nouns

Nihon	Japan
toshokan	Library
Tōkyō to ōta *ku*	Ota City, Tokyo Metropolis
doko	Where

Pronouns

A pronoun is a word that can function by itself as a noun, and that refers either to the participants in the discussion (*e.g.,* I, you) or to someone, or something mentioned previously (*e.g.,* she, it, this).

<u>*Question Pronouns*</u>

Here are the primary question words; see more in *ko, so a do* below.

dou	How	*itsu*	When
ikutsu	How many	*dare*	Who
ikura	How much	*naze*	Why
nan / nani	What	*doushite*	Why

KO SO A DO

Ko-so-a-do is the nickname for a group of words used to refer to items.

The following table shows the *ko-so-a-do* words. The prefix indicates the position relative to the speaker.

Prefix →	ko~	so~	a~	do~
Tail ↓	Closer to speaker	Closer to listener	Distant from both	Question
~re	kore this one	sore that one	are that one over there	dore what one?
~no *	kono this	sono that	ano that over there	dono What?
~nna	konna like this	sonna like that	anna like that over there	donna How?
~ko	koko here	soko there	asoko over there	doko Where?
~chira	kochira this direction (Formal)	sochira that direction (Formal)	achira that direction over there (Formal)	dochira which way? (Formal)

For instance, *ano* means that thing not near either party.

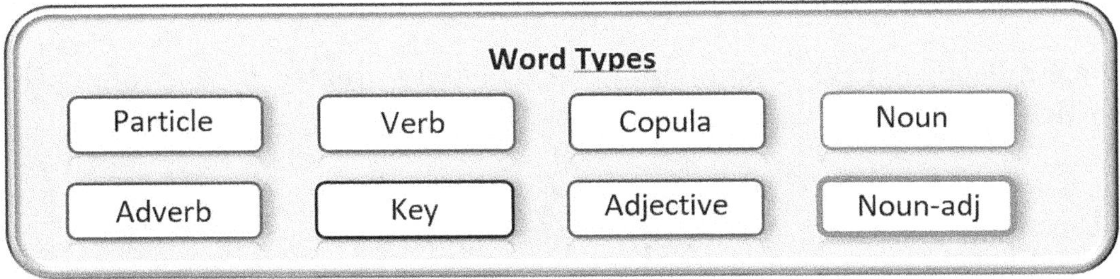

Noun-adj

Noun-adjs are usually called *na* adjectives. They are special nouns that are only adjectives when followed by *na*; the rest of the time they are simply nouns. We choose to call them noun-adjs, to remind ourselves that they are nouns that are adjectives only when *na* is added.

Noun-adjs can serve as nouns or adjectives. Consider the following:

As Noun	As noun-adj
nigiyaka desu lively is	*nigiyaka na hito* lively person
nigiyaka de wa ari masen Lively is not	*nigiyaka na hito de wa ari masen* lively person is not
nigiyaka deshita lively was	*nigyaka na hito deshita* lively person was
nigiyaka de wa ari masen lively was not	*nigiyaka na hito de wa ari masen deshita* lively person not was

In the left-hand column, the adjective is used as a noun; in the right, as a noun-adj. Notice that the noun-adjs always followed by *na* when used as an adjective.

Nons as adjectives

Other nouns can also be used as adjectives by appending the particle *no*.

<u>Example</u>

ishi no uchi
stone house

Noun-adjs from adjectives

Some adjectives have a noun-adj form. They are created by appending the particle *na* to the word.

adjective	→	**Noun-adj**
atatakai	→	atataka na
chiisai	→	chiisa na
okashii	→	okashi na
ookii	→	ooki na

The adjective form is used for modifying abstract nouns, such as thoughts (*shisō)* or rights (*riken*).

<u>Examples</u>

<u>As adjective</u>	<u>As noun-adj</u>
ōkii nozoni	ōki na nozoni
Big idea	Big idea

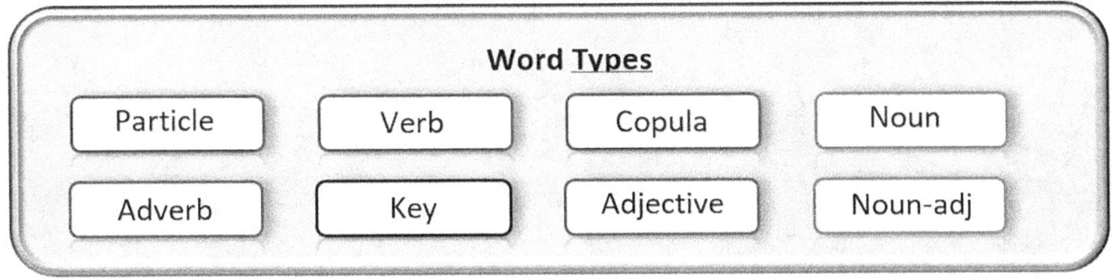

Changing word types

In the preceding text, we have seen how to change word types, such as using a verb as a noun. Here, for convenience, are the change opportunities.

Original	Append	To make
Verb	*koto or*	Noun
Adjective	*no*	
Noun	*no*	Adjective
Adjective	*na*	
Noun-Adj	*ni*	Adverb
Adjective	*ku*	

<u>Examples</u>

Verb to Noun	*hashiru* run	→	*hashiru no* running
Adjective to Noun	*abunai* dangerous	→	*abunai koto* danger
Adjective to Adjective	*ōkii* big	→	*ōki na* big
Noun to Adjective	*ishi* stone	→	*ishi no (kabe)* stone (wall)
Noun-Adj to Adverb	*genki* health	→	*genki ni* healthy

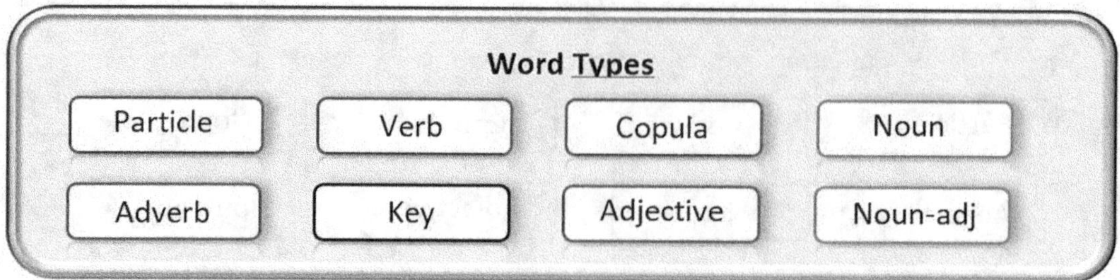

Takeaways

There are eight types of words used in Japanese. Particles identify the role of noun phrases.

Adverbs are words that can modify verbs. Verbs describe the action in a sentence.

Keys define the form of a sentence. Some keys define the case, others the mode of a verb.

Copulas couple a sentence subject to one of its attributes or to a state of being. Different copulas are used for properties and states of being.

Adjectives contain a hidden informal copula.

Nouns are names of things – either real or imaginary. Included in this word type are pronouns, times, locations, *etc.*

Noun-adjs are nouns that can serve as adjectives.

Except for the few irregular verbs and copulas, words are not changed for tense or other reasons. The tail is changed for verbs and adjectives.

Chapter 2-3
PHRASE TYPES

A PHRASE CONTAINS A WORD AND ITS MODIFIERS. For instance, 'big brick house on a hill' is a noun phrase; 'house' is the noun, and 'big' and 'brick' and 'on a hill' are its modifiers. Phrases are used as sentence elements. One exception: the tag phrase is not a true phase; it is a holder for after sentence words.

A Reminder about Word Order

There is one restriction in word order; words that modify other words must precede the modified word. That means an adjective must come immediately before a noun it is modifying, and an adverb must come before – though not necessarily immediately – the verb it is modifying. It also means that there are no subordinate clauses.

Display

In this chapter, phrases are shown as below:

Japanese
English
Phrase Name

The Japanese words are in *Romaji*. The English translation is word-for-word with the Japanese, except for topics, where "As for ..". is used.

<u>Example</u>

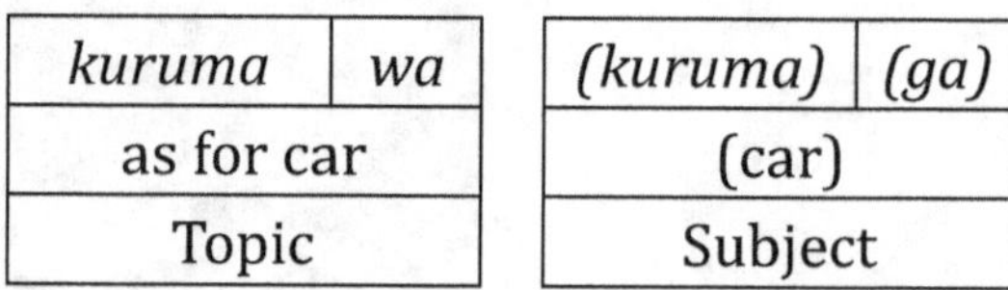

kuruma	*wa*		*(kuruma)*	*(ga)*
as for car			(car)	
Topic			Subject	

Since the topic is not a grammatic part of the sentence, a blank column separates the topic from the sentence. Words that are understood to exist but are not said or written are shown in parentheses.

A divider is between the noun and particle in noun phrases, between the verb and keys in verb phrases, and between the property and copula in copula phrases.

Noun	Particle		Verb	Keys		Property	Copula
Noun			Verb			Copula	

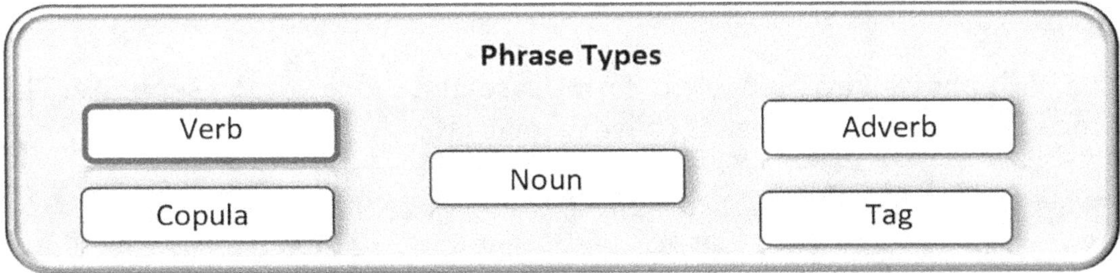

Verb Phrases

The verb phrase describes the action of the subject. It contains the verb and one or more keys to express the form, *i.e.,* the case (tense, polarity, and formality) and mode (command, able-to, want, *etc.)* of the action. The verb phrase serves as the verb of the sentence. It is a mandatory part of an action sentence. We will see later that negative verb phrases ae considered to be copula phrases.

A verb phrase consists of a verb and one or more keys:

Verb	Keys
Verb Phrase	

Note: Because Japanese is traditionally written without spaces between words, people often think some words are one word when they are two or more. For instance, *tabe mashita* is two words: the verb *tabe* and the key *mashita*. It is important to make this distinction.

Forms

The verb phrase keys define the form (case and mode) of the sentence. The process of defining the form is called formation.

<table>
<tr><th colspan="4">Form</th><th></th><th>Mode</th></tr>
<tr><td colspan="3">Case</td><td></td><td>Able-to</td></tr>
<tr><td>Polarity</td><td>Tense</td><td>Formality</td><td></td><td>Cause-Let</td></tr>
<tr><td rowspan="4">Positive</td><td rowspan="2">Non-Past</td><td>Informal</td><td></td><td>Command</td></tr>
<tr><td>Formal</td><td></td><td>Receiving</td></tr>
<tr><td rowspan="2">Past</td><td>Informal</td><td></td><td>Let's</td></tr>
<tr><td>Formal</td><td></td><td>If-Then</td></tr>
<tr><td rowspan="4">Negative</td><td rowspan="2">Non-Past</td><td>Informal</td><td></td><td>If-Once</td></tr>
<tr><td>Formal</td><td></td><td>If-Context</td></tr>
<tr><td rowspan="2">Past</td><td>Informal</td><td></td><td>If-Always</td></tr>
<tr><td>Formal</td><td></td><td>(More)</td></tr>
</table>

Formation Process

Verb Phrase Formation Process

Verb Group	Verb	Tail		Key
1	No Change	*	+	*
2				
3	*	Omit		

* depends on the Form

The process of forming a verb phrase begins with the Dictionary (informal positive non-past) form of the verb.

Verb

For Group 3 verbs only, replace the verb according to the form. For groups 1 and 2, the verb does not change.

Tail

For Group 1 verbs, the tail is changed according to the category associated with the form, using the Group 1 Tail Replacement Table (next page). Except for the *te* category, observe that the category represents the new vowel of the tail *hiragana* character. For instance, if the category is e, the tail *ku* becomes *ke*, *tsu* becomes *te*, etc.

For Groups 2 and 3 verbs, the tail (*ru*) is discarded.

Key

Append the key according to the form.

The key is either an *adjective* or a group 2 verb. It may in turn be formed by the same process. For instance, one can start with 'eat' (*tabe*) and find the potential form 'able to eat' (*tabe rareru*). The *rareru* can be formed for past tense – 'was able to eat"- the result is *tabe rare masen.*

Using the Verb Phrase Formation Table
(The table is on the next page)

Form: Select the row in the left-hand column for the desired form.

Verb For group 3 verbs only, discard the tail (*ru*) and replace the verb with the value in the Verb column for the verb.

Tail

Group 1 Verb: In the Group 1 Tail Category column and the Form row, find the Tail Category. Use the Group 1 Tail Replacement Table to find the new tail. Find the Dictionary Form tail in the table and move up or down to the row specified by the Tail Category to find the new tail.

Note that this is simply replacing the vowel part of the *hiragana* character for the dictionary form. For instance, if the dictionary form is *kiku*, the tail is *ku*. For the informal non-past negative form, the tail category is *a*. Replace the tail *ku* with *ka.*

Group 2 Verb: Discard the tail.

Group 3 Verb: Discard the tail.

Key: append the key from the selected row.

The result is a Verb Phrase.

In a few cases, there is a separate key for Group 1 and 2 verbs. Notice that the shorter key goes with the Group 1 verbs, which have a tail. You could think of the *ra* in *rareru* and the *sa* in *saseru* as being the new tail for the verb. I like the idea but could find nothing to support this view.

Note that the key can be further formed. For instance, if the mode is want, it can be made negative as

tai -> taku ari masen

or made past tense as

tai -> ta mashita

Verb Phrase Formation Process

Verb Type	Verb	Suffix	+	Key
Group 1	No Change	use table	+	use table
Group 2		Omit		
Group 3	use table			

Form			Verb — 3		Suffix 1*	Key 1 & 3	Key 2
		Group >	*kuru*	*suru*			
Informal	**Positive**	Non-Past	no change				
		Past	*ki*		*i*	*ta*	
	Negative	Non-Past	*ko*		*a*	*nsi*	
		Past	*ko*		*a*	*nakatta*	
Formal	**Positive**	Non-Past	*ki*	*shi*	I	*masu*	
		Past	*ki*	*shi*	I	*mashita*	
	Negative	Non-Past	*ki*	*shi*	a	*masen*	
		Past	*ki*	*shi*	a	*masen deshita*	
Desire						*tai*	
Volitional					I	*yo***	
Passive			*ko*	*sa*	a	*rareru*	*reru*
Causative			*ko*	*sa*	a	*saseru*	*seru*
Imperative				*shi*	e	*ro*	
Potential			*ki*	*deki*	e	*rareru*	*ru*
te			*ki*	*shi*	Omit	*te*	

* Group 1 see table next page - Groups 2 & 3: omit tail
** more commonly used in formal form - *mashyo*

Category			Group 1 Tail Replacement Table								
	a	*a*	*ka*	*ga*	*sa*	*ta*	*na*	*ba*	*ma*	*rq*
	i	*i*	*ki*	*gi*	*shi*	*chi*	*ni*	*bi*	*mi*	*ri*
Dictionary	u	*u*	*ku*	*gu*	*su*	*tsu*	*nu*	*bu*	*mu*	*ru*
	e	*e*	*ke*	*ge*	*se*	*te*	*ne*	*be*	*me*	*re*
	o	*o*	*ko*	*go*	*so*	*to*	*no*	*bo*	*mo*	*ro*
te form	te	*t*	*i*	*i*	*shi*	*t*	*n*	*n*	*n*	*t*

Instructions: Find the Dictionary Form tail in the u row.
Move up or down in the same column to the row designated by the Tail Category in the Formation Table to find the new tail.

Exception

An exception in the *te* form is the verb *iku (go)*. The *te* form is *itte*, not *iite* that the tables produce.

Spelling/Pronunciation

In English, we change some words to make it easier for the tongue. For instance, we say "**a** house" but "**an** old house," because it rolls off the tongue more readily than "**an** house" or "**a** old house". Japanese also change words for the same reason. In this chapter, we are combining words into phrases and often run into the need to make it easier to say. Here are some cases where spelling is changed:

Verb body ending sound	*a*	*n*	*a, i, u, e, o*
Followed by auxiliary starting with	*a*	*t*	*t*
Change	*a a → a wa*	*t→d*	*t→tt*
Example	*ka anai → ka wanai*	*sun te→ sun de*	*fu te → fu tte*

Negative Forms

Negative forms do not have any action. They state that something is <u>not</u> happening. The key is an adjective instead of a verb. Thus, negative forms are not verb phrases, they are copula phrases, described in the next section.

About keys

Modifiers always precede the word they are modifying. Accordingly, the verb is modifying the key. In the phrase *tabe mashita,* it is misleading to think the subject ate something, and did it in the past. It is better thought of as the subject did something in the past and that something was eat. Keys can be formed in the same manner as any other verb or adjective.

<u>Examples</u>

yasai	*o*	*tabe*	*sase*	*nakatta*
vegetables		eat	Cause-let	did not
Dir Obj		Verb		

Begin with (subject) *nakatta* – subject did not. Not what?
Next is *sase-* (subject) did not cause. Cause what?
Next is *yasui o tabe* – eat vegetables.
Subject was not caused to eat vegetables.

Notice that *saseru* was in turn formed as *sase nakatta.*

Subject is not always what you think!

The subject of a potential mode sentence is not the person with the ability; it is the thing one is able to do.

<u>Example</u>

ocha	*ga*	*nome*	*ru*
tea		drink	**able to**
Subject		Verb	key

The basic sentence is the subject and the last *ga ru,*" "*tea able to*". The verb *nomi* (drink) modifies *seru* and says what is able to be done. This is different from English – where the focus is on the person (**I** am able to drink tea); in Japanese, the focus is on the subject: for me, tea is able to be drunk.

We will find this difference in other forms. It is due, at least in part, to the teaching that says your identity is that of the group, not as an individual. So instead of drawing attention to yourself, you focus on the subject. We see this in the formation of want:

<u>Example</u>

ringo	*ga*	*tabe*	**tai**
apple		eat	**desirable is**
Subject		Verb	key

tai is an adjective that says the property of the subject is inducing the desire to do what the verb says. In this case, the apple causes the speaker to want to eat it. This is not to say the apple has some power, but that it inspires a sense of desire in the subject.

By the way, *tai* is an adjective because there is no action – the sentence is describing a state. So, this is a copula, not verb – phrase.

te Form

The *te* form is a versatile form for verbs. Its purpose is to link verbs and adjectives. *te* becomes *de* when following a verb ending in *n* (as in *yon de . . .*).

<u>Adjectives</u> - the *te* form of noun-adjs is formed by appending *de*. For adjectives, replace the final *i* with *kute*.

<u>Examples</u>

noun-adjs   adjectives

genki de		*yūmē de*		*taka kute*		*atsu kute*
healthy		famous		tall		hot
Noun-Adj		Noun-Adj		Adjective		Adjective

Connecting form

Ongoing action – the *te* form of a verb linked to *iru* is used to change a verb to relate continuing action. This is a state of being. *iru* can be further formatted. It is a copula form, which we will visit in the next section of this chapter.

Examples

Informal Formal	yon	de	iru	
			i	masu
	read	ing	is	
	Copula			

Request - Use the *te* form of a verb linked to *kudasai* (please) to request something. It is only used as formal mode.

Examples

tabe	te	kudasai.
eat		please
Verb		Verb

ma	tte	kudasai.
Wait		please
verb		Verb

Linking Adjectives - When two or more adjectives are used together, all but the last must be *te* form, to connect it to the following adjective. The *te* form of *genki* (a *noun-adj*) is *genki de)*.

Example

ōkiku	*te*	genki	*de*	tanoshii	hito
big		healthy		happy	person

Linking verbs - Use the *te* form to combine multiple verbs in one sentence.

Examples

Informal Formal	Kōbe	ni	i	tte	gyūniku	o	taberu	
							tabe	masu
	Kōbe to		go and		beef		eat	do

Go to Kōbe and eat beef

<u>Link sentences</u> - Use the *te* form to join two sentences. Note that *iru/ i masu* is shared by each sentence.

<u>Examples</u>

Informal Formal	tabete	no nde	iru i masu
	eating and	drinking	

<u>surround</u>

Some nouns describe actions and can be converted to verb phrases by adding *suru* (do). For instance, *unten* is a noun that means the operation of something (like a car). There is no verb 'to drive.' *unten suru* means 'operation do.' So, we can say

kuruma	o	unten	shi	masu
car		operate	do	

Of course, these words can be used as ordinary nouns. For instance, *benkyō* means study:

benkyō	o	shi	masu
study		do	

Nouns that can be used as verbs in this manner are generally borrowed words from Chinese and are written in *kanji* only in case you care!

The following is a sample of words that can be used with *suru:*

undō	exercise	*ryokō*	travel, make a trip
benkyō	study, diligence	*ryōri*	cook
denwa	phone call	*shigoto*	work
genshō	decrease, reduction	*sotsugyō*	graduate
koshō	be broken	*shokuji*	have a meal

<u>Examples</u>

denwa	shi masu
Phone call	do

ryori	suru
cook	do

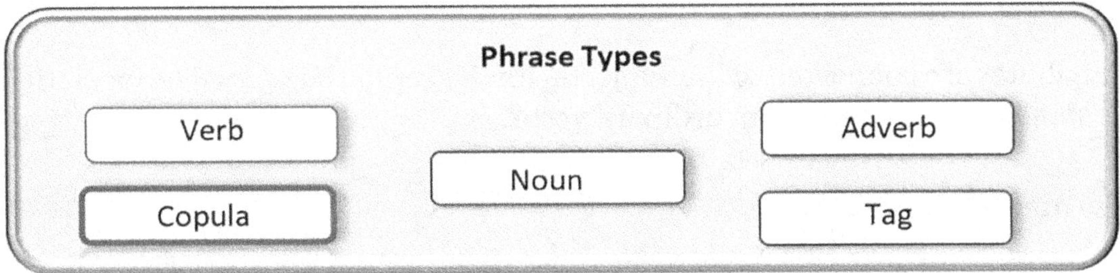

Copula Phrase

A copula phrase is a phrase that couples some property to the sentence subject. The property may be an attribute or a state of being of the subject. The phrase contains a property described by a noun or adjective or verb phrase and a copula to couple it to the subject:

Property	Copula
Copula Phrase	

Throughout this section, informal and formal terms are shown as

informal/formal.

In English, the copula 'be,' in its many forms (is, was, were, are, am, *etc.*) is the copula. It applies to attributes as well as states of existence. Not so in Japanese: there are three basic copulas – *da, aru,* and *iru* (and their formal equivalents – *desu, ari masu,* and *i masu*). Each depends on the type of property.

Properties

Property types are in two categories: attributes and states..

Property Type			**Copula**
Attribute	Noun		*dd/desu*
	Adjective		*none/desu*
State	Existence	Inanimate subject	*aru/ari masu*
		Animate subject	*iru/i masu*
	Ongoing		Verb-*te iru/i masu*
	Negative		Verb (neg form)

Attribute Property

Attributes are connected to the subject with the copula *da/desu*. The formation is somewhat different from ordinary verbs.

Formation of *da/desu*

Formation of da/desu

	Informal		Formal	
	Non-past	**Past**	**Non-past**	**Past**
Positive	*da*	*da tta*	*desu*	*de shita*
Negative	*de wa nai*	*de wa nakatta*	*de wa masen*	*de wa masen deshita*

The *te* form of *da* is *de.* Do not confuse it with the particle *de.*

<u>de wa</u>

Notice that the negative form of *da/desu* includes *de wa.* What is that all about?

<u>Example</u>

Negative

kore	*ga*	*ringo*	*de*	*wa*	*ari*	*masen*
This		apple	as for being		is	not
Subject		Copula Phrase				

One is tempted to say "*ringo ga ari masen*". That would mean "apples exist not," or "there are no apples". There may be apples, but we are talking about the subject. We need to say the subject is not an apple. Consider *ringo da wa,* which means "as for apple is," or "as for being an apple". This can serve as the property of the copula phrase. We must change *da* to the *te* form *de* to connect it to the copula *nai.* The complete copula phrase is then "*ringo de wa nai/ari masen*". So, we have "(subject) *ringo de wa nai/de wa ari masen,*" "(subject) as for being apple is not," or" this is not

<u>ja</u>

de wa is often shortened to *ja: "ringo ja ari masen".*

Formation of Adjectives

Adjectives can also be used as copula and can be formed.

Formation of Adjectives

	Informal				Formal			
	Non-past		**Past**		**Non-past**		**Past**	
	Tail	**Key**	**Tail**	**Key**	**Tail**	**Key**	**Tail**	**Key**
Positive	*i*	-	-	*katta*	*i*	*desu*	-	*katta desu*
Negative	*ku*	*nai*	*ku*	*nakatta*	*ku*	*ari masen*	*ku*	*ari masen deshita*

The adjective does not change – only the tail changes and a key are added.

An adjective cannot modify another adjective. Since the negative keys are adjectives, the adjective being formed is changed to an adverb by replacing its tail with *ku.*

Example

chisai	*nai*
Small	not
Adjective	Adjective

⟹

chisaku	*nai*
smally	not
Adverb	Adjective

Invalid   Valid

Attributes

The attribute may be color, owner, size, weight, *etc.,* and may be an adjective or noun phrase.

Examples

Copula Phrases

Noun formal	Aka desu	Red is
Noun formal	Nihonjin desu	Japanese is
Adjective formal	*chisai desu*	small is
Adjective informal	*ōkii*	big is
Noun phrase formal	*watashi no masen*	Mine is not
Adjective Informal	*ureshii*	Happy is
Adjective formal	*kanashi desu*	Unhappy is

A reminder that adjective means the body without its *i* tail. An informal sentence with an adjective as the property does not require a separate copula; you can think of the adjective as continuing a 'hidden *da.*' In this case the adjective retains its *i* tail.

<u>Examples</u>

au	*da*
blue	is

tanoshi	*desu*
fun	is

tanoshii
fun is

dō	*desu*
copper	is

State

Informal

genki	*da*
healthy	is
Copula Phrase	

Noun-adj

chisaii
small is
Copula Phrase

Adjective

watashi no	*nai*
mine	is not
Copula Phrase	

Noun

Properties

A subject may be described as being in a state of existence. This state may be simple that it exists or that it exists in a certain location or at a certain time, or in some state of activity, or state of inactivity.

<u>*State of Existence of Inanimate Subject*</u>

Inanimate subjects are anything that is not a living animate subject. States of existence of an inanimate subject use the copula *aru*. The formation is slightly different from group 2 verbs.

Formation of aru/ari masu

Formation of *airu/ari masu*

	Informal		Formal	
	Non-past	**Past**	**Non-past**	**Past**
Positive	*aru*	*a tta*	*ari masu*	*ari mashita*
Negative	*nai*	*nakatta*	*ari masen*	*ari masen deshita*

Inanimate objects may simply exist or exist in a certain place or time.

<u>Examples</u>

osake arimasu	There is sake
heya no naka ni i masu	Room in is
uchi no naka ni ari masen	House in is not
Kinō kuruma wa aki ari mashita	Yesterday car here was

State of Existence of Animate Subject

Animate subjects include only living animals that are animate. This includes all live animals, including humans. States of existence of an animate subject use the copula *iru.* The formation is slightly different from group 2 verbs.

Formation of iru/i masu

Formation of *iru/i masu*

	Informal		Formal	
	Non-past	**Past**	**Non-past**	**Past**
Positive	*i ru*	*i tta*	*i masu*	*i mashita*
Negative	*ira nai*	*i nakatta*	*i masen*	*i masen deshita*

States pf inanimate existence

Inanimate objects may simply exist or exist in a certain place or time.

<u>Examples</u>

Tokyo ni i masu	In Tokyo is
iru	Exists (lives)
Ofisu ni imasu	Office I is

State of Ongoing Action

Activity described by a verb may also be a state of ongoing action. *iru* is always used; *aru* is used for inanimate subjects which cannot have an ongoing state.

Examples

hashitte i maseu	running
katte iru	buying (shopping)
itte ii masu	going
isoide iru	hurrying

Negative State

Most would not think of this as a copula phrase. However, a negative key (*nai, masen, etc.*) is saying that a negative state exists, there is no action, and the sentence is relating the subject to that state.

Examples

no nai/i masen	not drink
no nde ii masen	not drinking
tabete i masen	not eating
nai	not exists
heya no naka ni ari masen	not in room

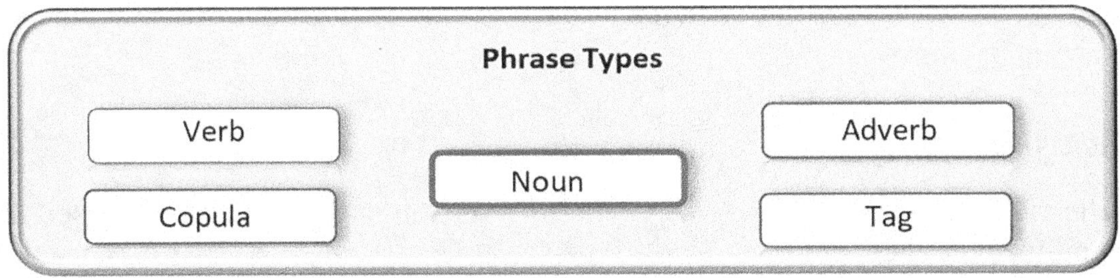

Noun Phrases

Noun phrases consist of a noun, modifiers, and an identifying particle. They. are used as the topic, subject, and direct and indirect objects in sentences. Modifiers are contained in an adjective phrase.

Adjective Phrase	Noun	Particle
Noun Phrase		

The adjective phrase contains modifying words. They can be simple or complex.

Complexity	Japanese	English
Simple	*uchi*	House
	ōkii uchi	Big house
	ōkiku te chairoi uchi	Big brown house
	Kenya san ga tateta ōkii uchi	Kenya built big house *i.e.,* big house that Kenya built.
Complex	*Kōbe ni sunde iru Kenya no tate ta ōkī uchi*	Kōbe lives in Kenya-built big house *i.e.,* big house that Kenya, who lives in Kōbe, built

The first is simply a noun with no adjective phrase. The second is a noun preceded by a simple adjective phrase containing a single adjective. The last is a noun modified by a complex adjective phrase.

Grammatic particles identify the role of the phrase in the sentence:

Phrase   **Particle**

Topic *wa*

Topic (also) *mo*

Subject *ga*

Indirect Object *ni*

Direct Object *o*

The verb phrase does not need a marker, it is identified by being the last in the sentence.

Adjective phrases

The modifiers can be adjectives, noun-adjs, or nouns. Adverbs may be used to modify adjectives.

A simple adjective phrase consists of one adjective.

<u>Example</u>

shiroi	*uchi*	*
white	house	*
Adjective	Noun	Particle
Noun Phrase		

*grammatic particle can mark the topic (*wa* or *mo*), subject (*ga*), or object (*ni* or *o*)

noun-adj – another simple phrase has only one noun-adj. It must be followed by *na*.

<u>Example</u>

genki	**na**	*kodomo*	*
healthy		child	*
noun-adj		Noun	Particle
Noun Phrase			

Noun as Adjective – a noun can be used as an adjective by appending *no*:

<u>Example</u>

ishi	*no*	*uchi*	*
stone		house	*
Adjective		Noun	Particle
Noun Phrase			

Adjective phrases may contain adverbs that modify adjectives in the phrase, so long as they are directly before the adjectives that they modify.

Example

totemo	oishii
very	delicious
Adverb	Adjective

Chained Adjectives – when two or more adjectives are used together the *te* form of the adjectives is used. The *te* form of an adjective is created by replacing the tail with *ku* and adding *te*: *chiisai → chīsakute.* The *te* form of a noun-adj is made by appending *de*, a form of *teyūmei → yūmei **de***

Example

tanoshi**ku**	*te*	*genki*	*de*	*chiisai*	*kodomo*	
happy		healthy		little	child	
adjective		noun-adj		adjective	Noun	Particle

Noun Phrase

NOTE: you cannot chain positive and negative adjectives:

~~oishii~~	to	~~chiisa~~	nai
delicious and (positive)		cheap is (negative)	

Adjective phrases

Adjective phrases are used in noun phrases to modify the noun. They may contain adverbs, so long as they are directly before the adjectives or nouns that they modify.

Examples

totemo	oishii
very	delicious
Adverb	Adjective

hayai	tori
early	bird
Adverb	Noun

English uses adjectives and following clauses to modify nouns; Japanese uses only adjective phrases that precede the noun. Converting clauses to adjective phrases is performed by first creating the clause as a sentence. Remember that all verbs in a sentence, except the last, are informal.

Consider the sentence

"I want to buy the house **that Kenya, who lives in Kōbe, built**".

The bold face words "that Kenya, who lives in Kōbe, built" modify 'house.' Clauses must be expressed as adjective phrases preceding the noun 'house.'

'There are two clauses:

that Kenya built – modifies house
who lives in Kōbe – modifies Kenya

To create an adjective phase, first make it into a sentence.

Kenya	ga	uchi	o	tate	ta
Kenya		house		build	did
Subject		Dir Obj		Verb	

Kenya built the house

Since house is what we are modifying, remove it to create the adjective phrase:

Kenya	ga	tate	ta
Kenya		build	did
Subject		Verb	

Convert Kenya to an adjective by replacing *ga* with *no:*

Kenya	no	tate	ta
Kenya		build	did
Adjective		Verb	

The second phrase is similarly created (we will visit adverb phrases shortly):

Kenya	ga	Kōbe	ni	sunde	iru
Kenya		Kōbe jn		live does	
Subject		Adverb		Copula	

Kenya lives in Kōbe.

Remove Kenya to make an adjective phrase, and use this to modify Kenya in the first phrase:

Kōbe	ni	sunde iru	Kenya	no	tate	ta
Kōbe in		lives does	Kenya		build did	
Adverb		Copula	Adjective		Verb	

This is the adjective phrase used to modify 'house.' It is shown here with the phrases that make it up.

Kōbe	ni	sunde	iru	Kenya	no	tate ta
Kōbe in		live does		Kenya		build did
Adverb Phrase		Copula Phrase		Adjective Phrase		Verb Phrase

Adjective Phrase
i.e., built by Kenya who lives in Kōbe

This phrase will become the direct object of a sentence.

Kōbe ni	sunde iru	Kenya no	tate ta	uchi	o
Adjective Phrase				Noun	Particle
Noun Phrase					

The *o* at the end is the particle identifying the phrase as the direct object.

Lists

Noun phrases my contain lists. There are three basic list types. They illustrate the use of particles in Phrases. Each boxed item is a noun phrase within the noun phrase.

Examples

Complete List

Aya san	to	Yuko san	to	Takumi san
Aya	and	Yuko	and	Takumi
Noun Phrase		Noun Phrase		Noun Phrase

Noun Phrase

to is an exclusive form of "and'

Partial List

ringo	ya	mango	ya	orenji	nado
apple	and	mango	and	orange	etc.
Noun Phrase		Noun Phrase		Noun Phrase	
Noun Phrase					

ya is an inclusive form of 'and.'

<u>Or List</u>

kōra	*ka*	*kōhī*	*ka*	*ocha*
cola	or	coffee	or	tea
Noun Phrase		Noun Phrase		Noun Phrase
Noun Phrase				

When used in a sentence, the last item needs a particle to identify the role of the list. For instance:

ringo	*ya*	*mango*	*ya*	*orenji*	*nado*	*ga*
apple	and	mango	and	orange	etc.	
Noun Phrase		Noun Phrase		Noun Phrase		Particle
Noun Phrase						

nado means '*etc.*' or 'and so forth.'

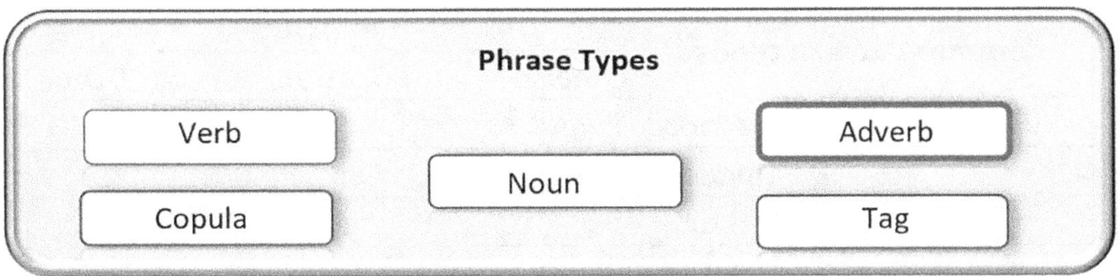

Adverb Phrase

The subject and verb are mandatory parts of a sentence. All the other parts of the sentence – direct and indirect objects and adverbs – help the verb. If you do not know what a part of a sentence is, it is most likely an adverb phrase. It can tell where and when an action took place. They can also describe amounts, means of action, and many other things.

Adverb phrases have many formats:

Various words
Adverb Phrase

Adjectives modify nouns, adverbs can modify verbs, nouns, adjectives, and other adverbs. An adverb phrase may simply contain one or more adverbs or may be complex.

<u>Examples</u>

tanoshiku	*uta*	*tta*
happily	sing did	
Adverb	Verb	

takusan	*sakana*
many	fish
Adverb	Noun

hijoni	*ōkī*
extremely	big
Adverb	Adjective

Now here is a surprise; adverb phrases do not always contain adverbs. Many are phrases that provide method, time, or location information about the verb without using adverbs. These phrases use particle markers to indicate the type of information.

Common Adverb types	Particle		
	Time	**Location**	**Other**
Duration	*kan*		
Destination		*ni*	
Direrction		*e*	
Means			*de*
With			*to*
At (place/time of action)	*de*	At (place/time of action)	
At (existence, no action)	*ni*	At (existence, no action)	
Start point	*kara*	Start point	
End point	*made*	End point	

Adverb phrases include statements of time, location, means, and other items that provide information about the verb.

<u>Examples</u>

At, From, and To locations and Means of Transport

ju nana ji	*made*
17 o'clock*	*to*
Adverb	

ju ni ji	*kan*
12hours	*duration*
Adverb	

Nagasaki	*ni*
Nagasaki **at**	
Adverb	

Fukaoka	**kara**
Fukaoka **from**	
Adverb	

Beppu	**made**
Beppu **to**	
Adverb	

densha	**de**
train **by**	
Adverb	

san ji	*ni*
3 o'clock	at
Adverb	

hachi ji	*kara*
8 o'clock	from
Adverb	

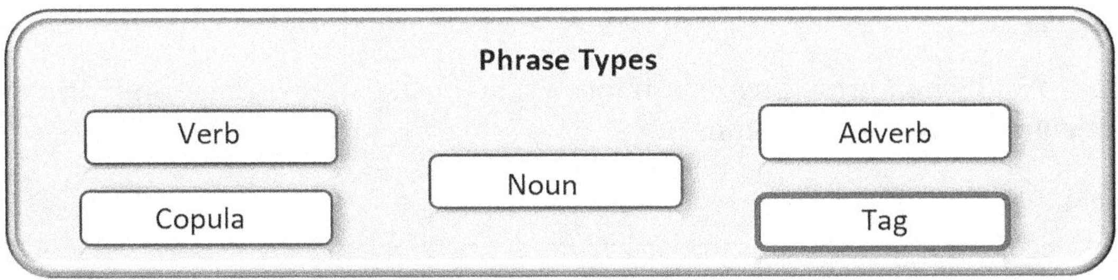

Tag Phrase

After a sentence, there may be one or more words that indicate different information about the sentence, *i.e.*, tells that the sentence is a question, has a certain mood, or has a continuation. These sentence endings are expressed in tag phrases.

Question	Mood	Connection
Tag Phrase	Tag Phrase	Tag Phrase

Question

ka changes the sentence into a question

<u>Example</u>

Question

Miyuki san,	*wa*	*daigakusei*	*desu*	**ka**
As for Miyuki		college student	is	?
Topic		Copula		**Tag**

Is Miyuki a college student?

Statement

Miyuki san,	*wa*	*daigakusei*	*desu*
As for Miyuki		college student	is
Topic		Copula	

Miuki is a college student

The two sentences appear identical, except the question version has *ka* appended. *ka* can be considered the same as a question mark (?).

Nuances

yo is used when providing new information, or like an exclamation mark, or for commands and invitations.

<u>Example</u>

kare	*ga*	*kochira*	*ni*	*kuru*	<u>**yo**</u>
he		this way		comes	**!**
Subject		Adverb		Verb	**Tag**

He comes this way!

---

ne is used frequently in casual situations. It is a way of expressing an opinion or feeling without being too assertive. It can also be used to confirm information

<u>Examples</u>

kyo	*wa*		*(kyo)*	*(ga)*	*atsui*	*desu*		**ne**
today			(today)		hot	is		**it**
Topic			Subject		Copula			**Tag**

It is hot today, isn't it?

kono kuruma	*wa,*		*(kono kuruma)*	*(ga)*	*takai*	*desu*		**ne**
As for this car			(this car)		expensive	is		**isn't it?**
Topic			Subject		Copula			**Tag**

This care is expensive, isn't it?

---

na is similar to *ne;* although not as assertive. As always, Japanese do not want to seem too assertive, and adding *na* to the end of a statement softens the impact.

<u>Example</u>

(kore)	*(ga)*	*hen*	*da*	*na*
(it)		Strange	is	**isn't it?**
Subject		Copula		**Tag**

It is strange, isn't it?

_no_ creates a question or adds emotional stress.

Example

(anata)	_(ga)_	_doko_	_ni_	_iki_		_**no**_
(you)		Where		Go		**?**
Subject		Adverb		Verb		**Tag**

Where (do you) go?

---

kana/kashira indicates uncertainty or wonder. _kana_ is used by males, _kashira_ by females

Example

kanojo	_wa,_		_(kanojo)_	_(ga)_	_kekkon_	_shite_	_iru_		_**kana**_
As for her,			(she)		married		is		**I wonder**
Topic			Subject		Verb				**Tag**

I wonder if she is married

Node at sentence end can be interpreted as 'because.'

Example

sono hon	_ga_	_muzukashii_		_node_		_yomi_	_masen deshita_	
That book		Difficutt is		because		read	not	did
Subject		Copula		Tag		Verb		

Because that book is difficult, (I) did not read (it).

_zo_ adds judgement to a sentence. Used only by males.

<u>Examples</u>

iku	_zo_
go	!
Verb	Tag

Go!

kono hako	_wa_	_(kono hako)_	_(ga)_	_omoi_	_zo_
As for this box,		this box		heavy is	!
Topic		Subject		Copula	Tag

This box is heavy!

Connections

soshite, sorekara – connects two sentences for sequential events

<u>Example</u>

Ota ku	_e_	_iki_	_mashita_	**soshite**
Ota City	to	go	did	**and**
Dir Obj		Verb		Tag

(I) went to Ota and ...

shikashi – However

<u>Example</u>

Nihon	_ga_	_daisuki_	_desu_	_shikashi_
Japan		lovable	is	however
Subject		Copula		Tag

Japan is lovable but ...

mata – Also

Example

Nihongo	o	hanashi	masu		mata
Japanese		speak			also
DirObj		Verb			Tag

(I) speak Japanese and ...

sono toki – At that time – then

Example

Ōta ku	e	i	ta		sono	toki
Ota City to		go	did		at that time	
Adverb		Verb			Tag	

When I went to Ota ...

b□i wa – If you or If this happens

Example

kaji	no		b□i	wa
fire			if happens	
Adverb			Adverb	

If there is a fire ...

dakara – So

Example

$ 2,500	de	kachi	mashita		dakara
$ 2,500		win	did		so
Adverb		Verb			Tag

(I) won $2,500 so . . .

Other Particles

Many other particles can be used to make verb phrases for various purposes.

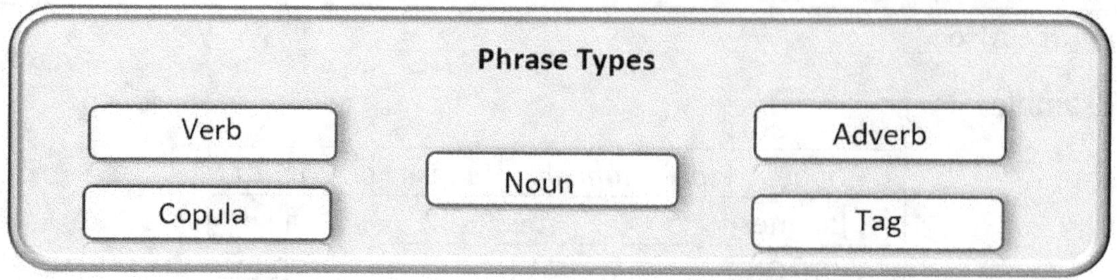

Chaining word types

Here is a summary of the methods for chaining words.

Nouns

Connect each to the next with *to* (and):

Yoko san	to	Midori san	to	Kaya san
Yoko	and	Midori	and	Kaya

Noun-adjs

Connect each to the following with the *te* form:

yume	de	genki	de	kyoushitu
famous	and	healthy	and	silent

Adjectives

Connect each to the following with the *te* form:

takaku	te	furuku	te	Kirei
Tall	and	old	and	pretty

Mixed adjectives

Connect each to the following with the *te* form:

yume	de	furuku	te	kyoushitu
famous	and	old	and	silent

Closed list of nouns

Same as connected nouns

A	to	B	To	C
A	**and**	**B**	**and**	**C**

Or list of nouns

Connect to next in list with *ka* (or)

A	ka	B	ka	C
A	or	B	or	C

Open list of nouns

Connect to next in list with *ya*, end list with *nado* (etc.)

A	ya	B	ya	C	nado
A	and	B	and	C	

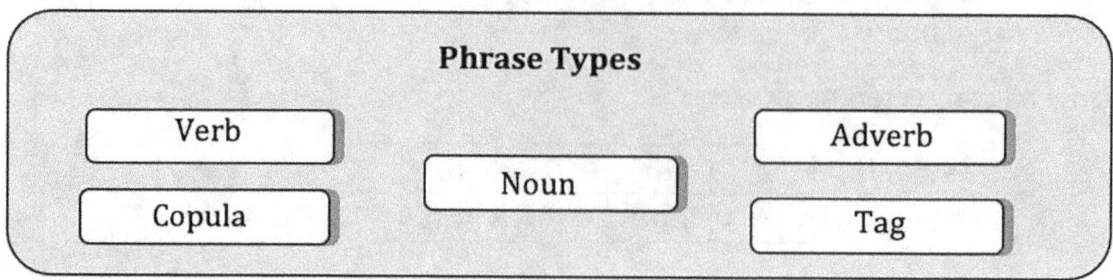

Takeaways

Phrases are groups of words that serve as part of a sentence. There are five Phrase types.

A verb phrase contains a verb and optional keys that define the form of the sentence. The tail of the verb changes according to the form, and a key is added to define the form. The key may in turn have a key to define the case of the verb phrase (*e.g., reri masen.*).

A copula phrase contains either a noun or noun-adj defining the property of the sentence subject and a copula, or an adjective that defines the property and provides an informal copula.

A noun phrase contains a noun, modifiers for the noun, and a particle identifying the role of the phrase.

An adverb phrase contains words to modify a verb.

A tag phrase contains a particle that sets the mood of the sentence.

Chapter 2-5
ELEMENT TYPES

S ENTENCES ARE COMPRISED OF A SERIES OF ELEMENTS . Each has a role that is expressed as a phrase.

Display

In this chapter, elements are displayed as shown here:

Japanese
English
Element Name

Elements

Element	Role	Phrase Type
Topic	Introduction	Noun
Subject	Who or what did the action or is being described	Noun
Indirect Object	Who or what received the action	Noun
Direct Object	What was used in the action of the	Noun
Adverb	How the action was done	Adverb
Verb	The action	Verb
Copula	Property of subject matter	Copula
Tag	Extra information about Sentence	Tag

The topic element is an introduction to the sentence; not part of it.

The subject and verb or copula elements are required, otherwise the sentence is meaningless. However, the subject element is often virtual, *i.e.,* it is understood but does not appear in the sentence.

There may be many adverb elements to modify the verb element.

Element Order

It is often said that English is a SVO (subject – verb – object) language, while Japanese is a SOV language. But that is an over-simplification. It is possible to say

I am to New York going,
and

(watashi)	yomi	mashita	hon	o	Aya san	ni
(I))	read did		book		Aya to	
Subject	Verb		Dir Object		Indir Object	

I read the book to Aya

However, it is rare to place the verb anywhere other than the end in Japanese.

Whereas adjectives must come immediately before the nouns they affect and are therefore contained in a noun phrase, adverbs that modify a verb can appear almost anywhere in a sentence, so long as they precede the verb.

<u>Examples</u>

sugu	ni
Quickly	
Adverb	

kare	wa
As for him	
Topic	

(kare)	(ga)	mise	ni	hashi tta.
(He)		store to		ran
Subject		Adverb		Verb

kare	wa
As for him	
Topic	

(kare)	(ga)	mise	ni	sugu	ni	hashi tta.
(He)		store to		Quickly		ran
Subject		Adverb		Adverb		Verb

kare	wa
As for him	
Topic	

(kare)	(ga)	sugu	ni	mise	ni	hashi tta.
(He)		Quickly		store to		ran
Subject		Adverb		Adverb		Verb

Adverbs that modify other adverbs or adjectives must come immediately before the word they modify.

<u>Example</u>

kare	wa		(kare)	(ga)	totemo sugu	ni	mise	ni	hashi tta.
As for him			(He)		very quickly		store to		ran
Topic			Subject		Adverb		Adverb		Verb

You cannot say *"totemo kare sugu"* (very he quickly) in Japanese or in English.

The adverbs modifying the main verb may be separated within a sentence.

<u>Example</u>

kare	wa		sugu	ni	kare	ga	mise	e	tanoshiku	hashi tta
As for him,			quickly		(he)		store to		happily	ran
Topic			Adverb		Subject		Adverb		Adverb	Verb

Quickly he the store to happily ran

Sentence Structure

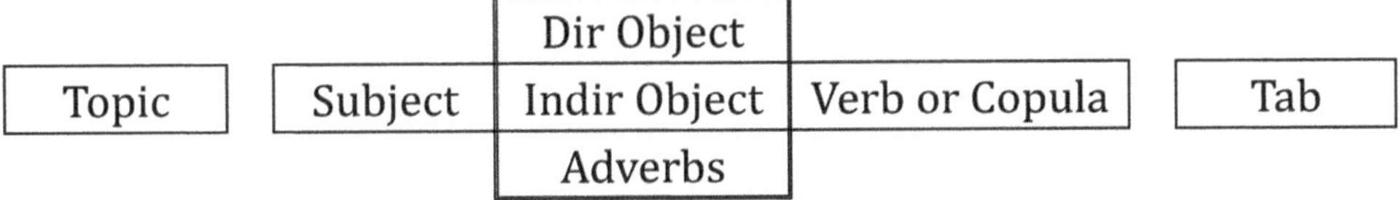

The basic sentence is the subject element and the verb or copula element. The object elements and adverb elements are modifiers for the verb element. The topic and tag elements are outside of the sentence.

One can argue that the indirect and direct object elements ae adverb phrases. It might be simpler to consider them as such. However, I have chosen to keep them as separate element types, partly because there may be many adverb elements, but there can only be one direct and one indirect object element, and partly because they are significant parts of the sentence.

Omitting Elements

Elements are often omitted when they are not necessary. While this is true in most languages, it is carried to an extreme in Japanese. Most omitted words are based on the idea that everyone knows what is omitted. Even though it is a grammatically mandatory part of the sentence, the subject element is frequently omitted.

Most references to self or to another are omitted. Instead of saying "I am Japanese" one simply says, "am Japanese". Instead of asking "what is your work?" one simply says "Work?" with *wa* to indicate that is the topic. And possessives are frequently omitted.

Another reason to omit elements is to avoid being blunt. In response to an invitation, one might answer "Sorry, tomorrow is a bit . . ". Even in English, we are likely to say "Tomorrow: Philadelphia," rather than

Tomorrow I am going to Philadelphia.

But it goes even farther in Japanese. The sentence's subject is omitted frequently, on the basis that it is already know by the listener. One avoids drawing attention to oneself by not starting a sentence with "I" instead of *"watashi wa Kyohei desu"* (I am Kyohei) one simply says *"Kyohei desu"* (am Kyohei).

It is often not necessary to use a possessive, nor to finish a question:

(a*nata no*) o*namae wa* (*nan desu ka?*)
(Your) name (what is?)

Repeated possessives and pronouns are omitted; instead of
"she went to her room, she changed her dress, she brushed her hair, and

she wrote in her diary

one might say

"She went to her room, changed clothes, brushed hair, and wrote in diary".

Even "her room" can become "room" if it is clear what room she went to.
As early as 604 CE, the "Seventeen Article Constitution" began with

"Harmony is to be valued and quarrels should be avoided".

To this day, it is important to maintain harmony and avoid conflicts. Accordingly, words may be omitted to avoid being too negative: "It is not impossible, but . . . (it will be very difficult)".

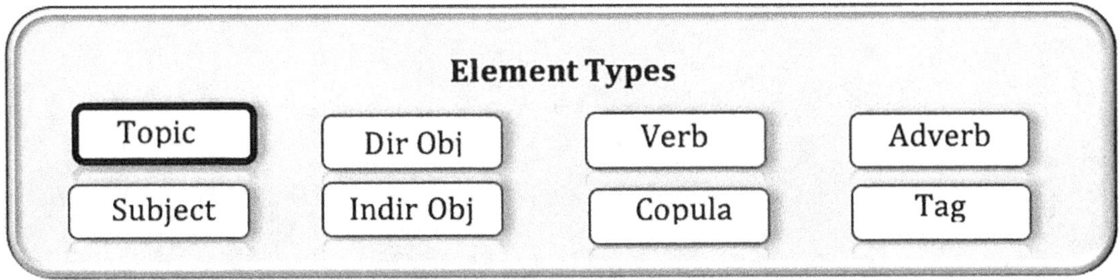

Topic Element

The topic element is a noun phrase marked by *wa* or *mo*. It is unique to the Japanese language. It serves as a preamble to the sentence but must not be considered part of the sentence; it is an introduction only. Most translate it as" As for . . ". or" Speaking of . .. " It is used to address a previous topic in the conversation.

<u>Example</u>

Miyu san	*wa,*		*(Miyu san)*	*(ga,)*	*daigakusei*	*desu*
As for Miyu,			(she)		college student is	
Topic			Subject		Copula	

The topic is 'Miyu san', the subject of the sentence is understood to be Miyu san or 'she,' the person in the topic, so it is not necessary to repeat the name. The alternate topic marker *mo* is an inclusive particle; it means 'also' or 'too,' whereas *wa* includes only the preceding noun. The topic marker was originally *ha* (は), but in time it became *wa*. It is still written as *ha*. Here we use the spoken form *wa*.

<u>Example</u>

Miyu san	*mo,*		*(Miyu san mo)*	*(ga,)*	*daigakusei*	*desu*
As for Miyu also,			(she also)		college student is	
Topic			Subject		Copula	

One way to think about topics is to make them separate sentences.

<u>Example</u>

(Topic) I will talk about Miu.
(Sentence) Miu is a college student.

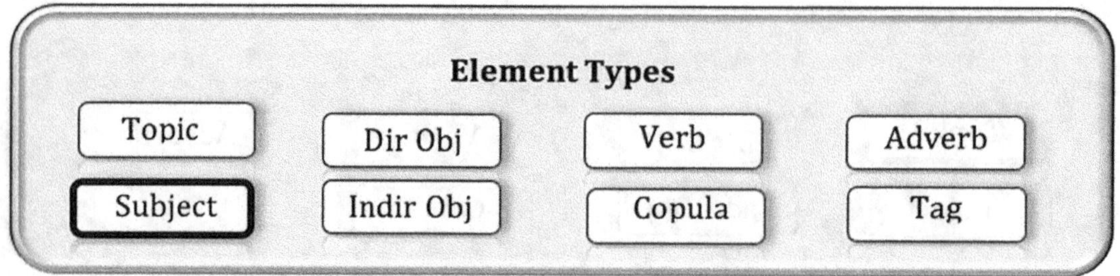

Subject Element

The subject element is a noun phrase marked by the particle *ga* in a descriptive sentence it identifies the thing that is being described. In an action sentence it identifies the thing that is performing the action described by the verb. In either case, it is a mandatory element. That said, it is rarely stated – it is usually a virtual subject; not written or said but understood by the speaker and listener either from the topic or from the ongoing dialog. Throughout this text, if it is not stated in the sentence it is shown in parentheses to remind us that it is mandatory and understood.

<u>Example</u>

Miyu san	*wa,*		*(Miyu san)*	*(ga)*	*daigakkosei*	*desu.*
As for Miyu,			**(she)**		college student is	
Topic			Subject		Copula	

The subject element of a sentence is a noun phrase identified by the particle *ga*, and the topic element is a noun phrase identified by the particle *wa* or *mo*. There are pages and pages of web sites and books trying to explain the difference between using *wa* and *ga*. It is not complicated. Only *ga* identifies a subject., and the subject is mandatory. Many people get this wrong. I can imagine a teacher saying "I have said '*watashi wa, sensei desu*' a zillion times," thinking *wa* is identifying the subject. What the person said is grammatically acceptable, but the explanation is wrong. The translation is

watashi	*wa,*		*(watashi)*	*(ga)*	*sensei*	*desu.*
as for me,			(I)		teacher am.	
Topic			Subject		Copula	

As for me, I am a teacher

watashi ga is a virtual subject for the sentence. It as if it is there, but you do not see or hear it.

Both topic and subject can be used in the same sentence.

<u>Example</u>

Nihon wa, Tokyo ga shuto desu
As for Japan, Tokyo is the capital

If a sentence has a topic and no subject, the subject is usually assumed to be the topic. It is also possible and frequently occurs, to have neither topic nor subject. We do this in English: "Eat", "Wonderful", "Going now". The subject is understood: **"You** eat," **"It** is wonderful," **"I** am going now". The same is true in Japanese: *"tabe ro* (eat)", *"subarashii"* (wonderful), "ima *itte i masu"* (Now going). Here are guidelines for subject and topic in a conversation:

Situation Use
Introducing a new Topic Subject
Returning to a previous Topic Topic
Emphasizing the Subject Subject

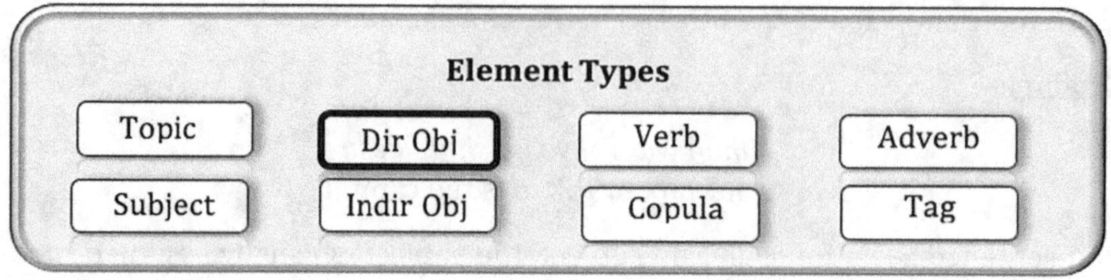

Direct Object Element

The direct object is a noun phrase marked by the particle *o*. It identifies the thing that the verb is acting on. in the following example, 'red apple' is the direct object:

<u>Example</u>

(watashi)	*(ga)*	*akai ringo*	*o*	*tabe*	*mashita*
(I)		**red apple**		eat	did
Subject		Dir Obj		Verb	

I ate a red apple

The direct object element marker particle is pronounced *o* but still written as the original *wo (を)*.

<u>Example</u>

Yoko san	*wa,*		*(Yoko sa)n*	*(ga)*	*watashi*	*ni*	*ringo*	*o*	*ageri*	*mashita.*
As for Yoko,			(Yoko)		me	to	apple		give	did
Topic			Subject		Ind Obj		Dir Obj		Verb	

Yoio gave to me an apple.

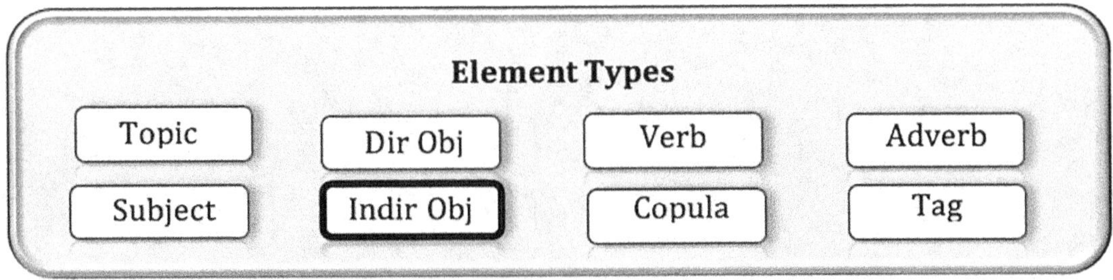

Indirect Object Element

The indirect object element is a noun phrase marked by the particle *ni*. It describes the recipient of the verb action. *ni* is the marker, which is consistent with its role as marking ends.

<u>Example</u>

Yoko san	*wa,*		*(Yokosan)*	*(ga)*	*wakashi*	*ni*	*ringo*	*o*	*ageri*	*mashita*
As for Yoko,			(Yoko san)		me	to	apple		give	did
Topic			Subject		Ind Obj		Dir Obj		Verb	

Yoko gave an apple to me

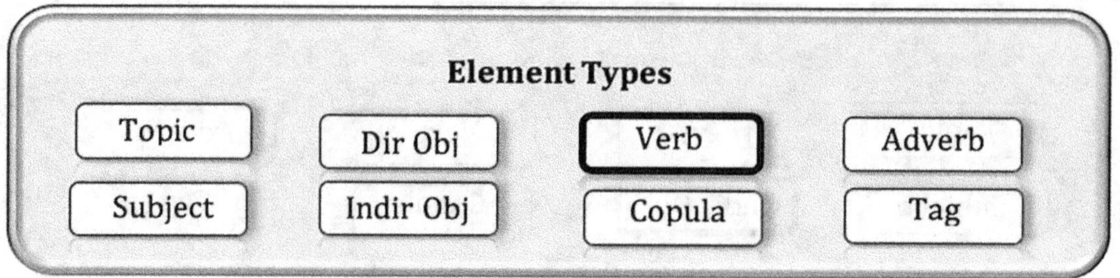

Verb Element

The verb element is a verb phrase used in action sentences. It describes an action off the subject. It is mandatory for action sentences.

<u>Example</u>

Miyuki	*wa,*
As for Miyuki,	
Topic	

(Miyuki)	*(ga)*	*Hiroki*	*ni*	*ringo*	*o*	*age*	*mashita*
(Miyuki)		Hiroki	to	apple		give	did
Subject		Ind Obj		Dir Obj		Verb	

Miyuki gave an apple to Hiroki.

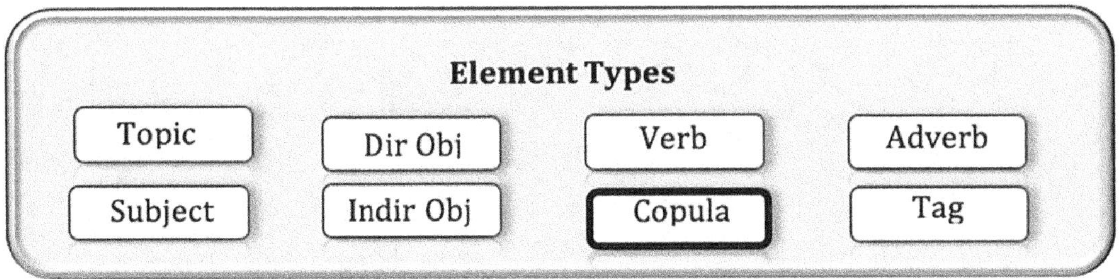

Copula Element

A copula element is a copula phrase. It contains a property of the subject, and a link (copula) to the subject.

<u>Examples</u>

ringo	*wa,*
As for the apple,	
Topic	

(ringo)	*(ga)*	***midori***	***desu***
(it)		**green**	**is**
Subject		**Copula**	

tatemono	*wa,*
As for the building,	
Topic	

(tatemono)	*(ga)*	***ōkii***	***(da)***
(it)		**big**	**(is)**
Subject		**Copula**	

In the first example, the copula *desu* couples the property (*midori*) to the subject (*ringo)*. In the second example, ōkii is an adjective that means "big is". The dictionary form copula (*da*) is contained in the adjective.

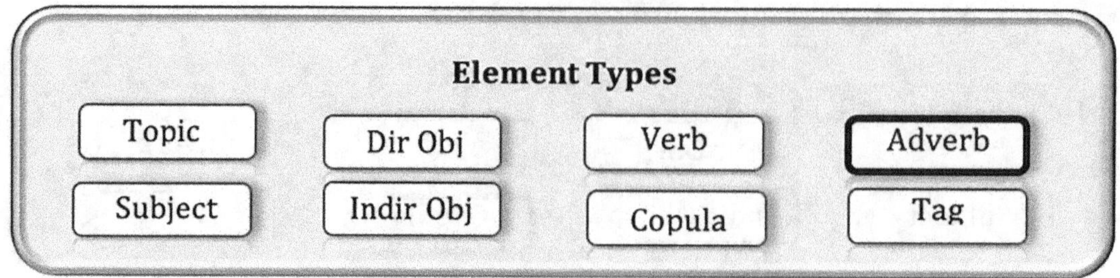

Adverb Element

Adverb elements are adverb phrases that modifies a verb. A sentence may contain more than one adverb element. They may appear anywhere in the sentence, so long as they precede the verb they are modifying.

<u>Examples</u>

watashi	*wa,*
As for me,	
Topic	

(watashi)	*(ga)*	*gakkō*	*ni*	*yukkuri*	*aruki*	*mashita.*
(I)		school	to	slowly	walk	did.
Subject		Abverb		Adverb	Verb	

I walked slowly to school.

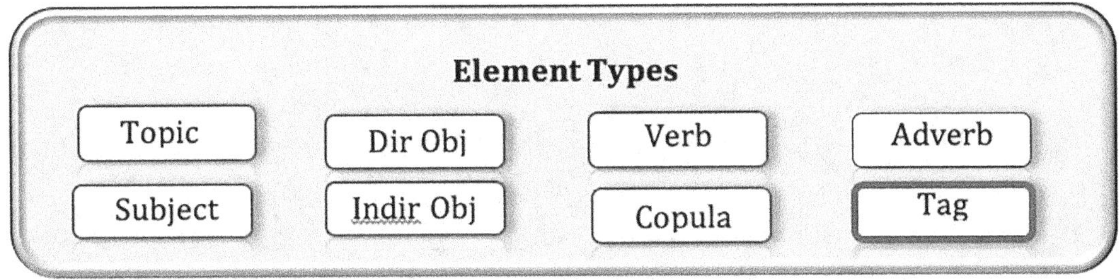

Tag Element

The tag element is a tag phrase at the end of the sentence. The tag adds a bit of information such as making the sentence into a question, indicating nuance. or connecting to another sentence. It is outside of the sentence.

<u>Examples</u>

anata	wa,
As for you,	
Topic	

(anata)	(ga)	dare	desu
(you)		who is	
Subject		Copula	

ka
?
Tag

Who are you?

(kore)	(wa)	ii otenki	desu
(it)		Good weather is	
Subject		Copula	

ne
is not it
Tag

Nuance: Good weather, isn't it?

(watashi)	ga	Tokkyo	e	iki	mashita	ga
(I)		Tokyo	to	go	did	but
Subject		Adverb		Verb		Tag

Connecting: I Tokyo to went

sukaitsuri	o	mi	masen	deshita
Sky Tree		see	not	did
DirObj		Verb		

Sky Tree (I) did not see

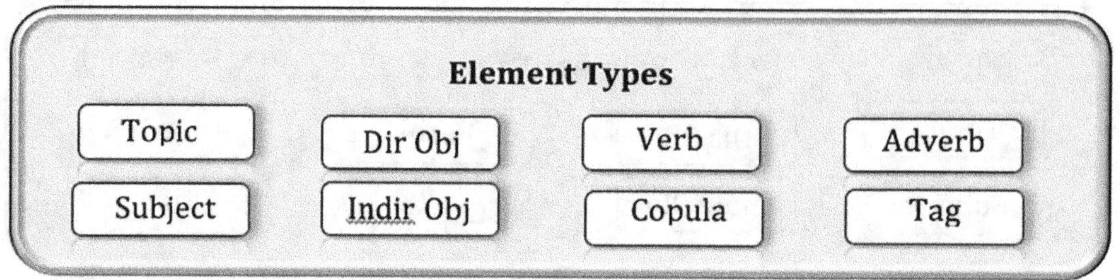

Takeaways

Sentences are composed of elements. Each Element is implemented as a phrase.

The Topic Element is a prelude to the sentence and not grammatically part of it. It identifies the topic addressed by the sentence. It is a Noun Phrase.

The Subject Element contains the thing that is acting. Every sentence has a subject, but often it is not present, it is a virtual subject, understood by all without being said or written. It is a Noun Phrase.

The Direct Object Element identifies the thing that is used in the action of the subject. It is a Noun Phrase.

The Indirect Object Element identifies the recipient of the action. It is a Noun Phrase.

The Copula Element identifies the property of the subject. It is a Copula Phrase.

The Verb Element identifies the action. It is a Verb Phrase.

The Adverb Element tells how the Verb is performed. It is an Adverb Phrase.

The Verb or Copula Element always at the end of the sentence (except for possible endings) is.

The Tag Element is a Tag Phrase that identifies the sentence as a question, or adds nuance, or provides a connection to a second sentence.

Chapter 2-6
SENTENCES

FINALLY WE GET TO THE POINT OF ALL THIS – making sentences. There are two types of sentences: action and description. Each is comprised of elements.

Action sentences describe the action of the subject, as described by the verb element modified by adverb and object elements.

Description sentences describe some property of the subject – it may be an attribute (*e.g.,* red or Miyuki's), or a state of existence. ('in the other room' or 'running'), or a state of not doing (negative sentence). The subject has the property described by the copula modified by objects and adverbs.

Display

In this chapter, diagram blocks represent elements. <u>Example</u>

watashi	*ga*
I	
Subject Element	

Tokyo	*ni*	*iki*	*masu*
Tokyo to		go	do
Adverb Element		Verb Element	

Element Order

In English, element order is important. Consider the following:

The cat	ate	the fish
Subject	Verb	Dir Obj

The cat ate the fish

The fish	ate	the cat
Subject	Verb	Dir Obj

The fish ate the cat

The order completely changes the meaning. However, in Japanese one can say

sakana	*o*	*neko*	*ga*	*tabe*	*mashita*
Fish		cat		eat	did
Dir Obj		Subject		Verb	

Fish cat ate

neko	*ga*	*sakana*	*o*	*tabe*	*mashita*
Cat		fish		eat	did
Subject		Dir Obj		Verb	

Cat ate fish

Thanks to the particle markers, both mean the same thing.

So long as the verb element is at the end and adverb elements precede the verb element, they modify, any order is acceptable.

Adverb elements may be anywhere before the related verb. Typically, if an adverb element is describing times related to the action, it can be at the very beginning. However, it may be placed anywhere before the verb element.

<u>Examples</u>

ku ji	*ni*
nine o'clock at	
Adverb	

watashi	*wa*
as for me,	
Topic	

(watashi)	*(ga)*	*Tōkyō ni*	*iki masu*	
(I)		Tokyo to	go	do
Subject		Adverb	Verb	

At nine o'clock I go to Tokyo

watashi	*wa*
as for me,	
Topic	

(watashi)	*(ga)*	*ku ji*	*ni*	*Tōkyō*	*ni*	*iki*	*masu*
(I)		Nine o'clock	at	Tokyo	to	go	do
Subject		Adverb		Adverb		Verb	

I at nine o'clock go to Tokyo

But – there can be a reason to use a specific order of elements. Let us use a more interesting sentence:

I went with Miyuki to see the movie 'Shogun' at the Ritz theater.

or

I went to the Ritz theater with Miyuki to see 'Shogun'

or

I saw 'Shogun' at the Ritz theater with Miyuki.

Each means the same thing, but the emphasis is different. The first features Miyuki; the movie is less important, and the theater is the least important. The second features the theater, and the third features the movie. In English, the importance of the elements decreases as the sentence progresses.

Surprise! In Japanese it is exactly the opposite. We get rid of the details before relating the main point. While it is correct to say the order of elements is not defined by grammar rules, it is also correct to say that the order can be important in emphasizing certain elements in the sentence.

<u>Examples</u>

(watashi)	*(ga)*	*Miyuki*	*to*	*ritsu*	*no*	*ēgakan*	*de*	*Shogun*	*no*	*ēgo*	*o*	*mi*	*mashita*
(I)		Miyuki with		Ritz theater at				Shogun		movie		see	did
Subject		Adverb		Adverb				Adverb				Verb and	

The emphasis is on the movie.

(watashi)	*(ga)*	*Shogun*	*no*	*ēgo*	*o*	*rittsuu*	*no*	*ēgakan*	*de*	*Miyuki*	*to*	*mi*	*mashita*
(I)		Shogun		movie		Ritz theater at				Miyuki	With	see	did
Subject		Dir Obj				Adverb				Adverb		Verb	

The emphasis is on Miyuki

The particles identifying the role of the phrases gives you freedom to arrange the element order any way you want. The elements are of increasing importance as the sentence progresses. Even the topic and subject can move; they do not have to be at the beginning of the sentence. But again, the verb element must be last, followed by optional tag elements.

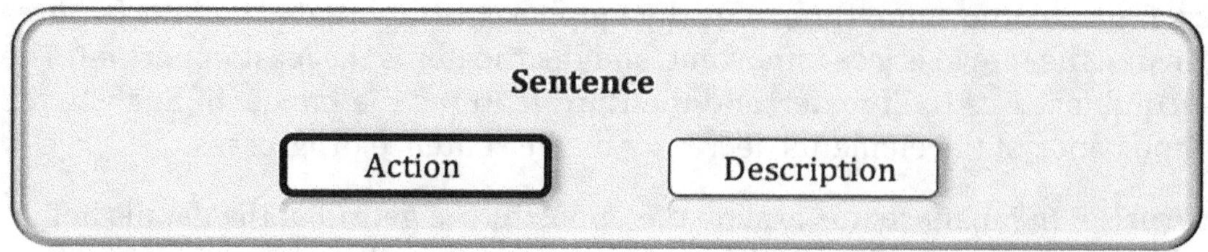

Action Sentences

An action sentence describes some action performed by the subject.

Introduction	Who Does	Does to	Does what	Ending
		Indirect Object		
		Does with		
Topic	Subject	Direct Object	Verb	Tag
		Does how		
		Adverb		

- The optional topic element is an introduction to the sentence. It is grammatically separate from the sentence.

- The mandatory subject element is the thing or person doing the action. Even though it is mandatory, it is often a virtual subject - understood but not written or said.

- The optional indirect object element is the recipient of the action.

- The optional direct object element describes the item with which the action is being performed.

- The optional adverb elements describe the time and/or location and/or way the action is performed.

- The mandatory verb element describes the action.

- The optional tag element describes the mood of the sentence or connects the sentence to another or defines the sentence as a question.

Example

Yoko san	wa	(Yoko san)	(ga)	tanoshi ku	Hoshino sensei	ni	hana	o	age	mashita
As for Yoko,		(Yoko san)		happily	Hoshino teacher	to	flower		give	did
Topic		Subject		Adverb	Indir Object		Dir Obj		Verb	

Yoko happily gave flowers to teacher Hoshino

In this example:

- The **topic** element announces that Yoko san will be discussed in the sentence.

- The **subject** element (*yoko san*), in this case silent but understood that Yoko performs the action,

- The **adverb** element (*tanoshiku* – happily) says how the action is performed,

- The **verb** element (*age mashita* – give did) describes the action,

- The **direct object** element (*hana* - flower) is what is acted upon, and

- The **indirect object** element (*Hoshino sensei* – teacher Hoshino) is the recipient of the action.

Example Sentences

In the following text, this shorthand is used:

T – topic element
S – subject element
I – indirect object element
D – direct object element
V – verb element

Non-past Tense

Informal Formal	watashi	wa	(watashi)	(ga)	kōhī	o	nomu / nomi masu
I			(I)		coffee		Drink
Topic			Subject		Dir Obj		Verb

Non-past tense describes an action that is not complete. For informal mode, the Dictionary Form is used.

Past Tense

Informal Formal	*watashi*	*wa*		*(watashi)*	*(ga)*	*sushi*	*o*	*tabe*	*ta* *mashita*
	I			(I)		sushi		ate	
	Topic			Subject		Dir Obj		Verb	

Past tense expresses an action that has completed.

Able to mode

hon	*ga*	*yome*	*ru*
book		read	is able
Subject		Verb	

Book is able to be read

The Able-to mode expresses something that the subject is capable of doing. In English, we would say the speaker is able to read the book. But the Japanese avoid speaking about people. Instead of saying "I can read the book," one says something like "for me, the book can be read". Some will tell you that in this case, *ga* is marking the object, not the subject. That is not the case. However, you can say *watashi wa hon o yume ru* – (I) it is possible (to) read (the) book. And that is why some believe – incorrectly – that *ga* can sometimes be an object marker.

Cause-Let mode

Cause-Let mode expresses something the subject of the sentence causes or allows another to do, or in the negative, prevents someone from doing. The basic form of the sentence is

S *ga* I *ni* V *saseru*
S is the subject and *saseru* is its verb
V is the action performed by indirect object I
Subject S is caused/allowed to do V

Example

Chiaki san	*ga*	*Ryoko san*	*ni*	*gohan*	*O*	*tabe*	*sase*	*ta*
Chiaki		Ryoko		rice		eat	cause/let	did
Subject Element		Indir Obj Elem		Dir Obj Elem		Verb Element		

Chiaki caused Ryoko to eat rice

Receiving mode

The receiving (usually called passive) mode states that the action of the verb is done to someone. It takes the emphasis off from who does the action, and places is on who is affected by the action. This mode focuses on the recipient of the verb action. *ni* marks the doer of the verb. The basic form of the sentence is similar to the cause-let form:

$$S\ ga\ I\ ni\ V\ rareru$$

S is the subject and *rareru* is its verb
V is the action performed by indirect object I
Subject S received the action of the verb V done by I

Example

sakana	*ga*	*neko*	*ni*	*tabe*	*rare*	*ta*
Fish		cat		eat	receive	did
Subject		Indir Object		Verb		

Fish did receive cat eat *i.e.*; the cat ate the fish

The main sentence is *sakana ga rare ta* - the fish receive did. Inside, *neko ni tabe* – cat by eat. The combination means fish by cat eat received – the fish received the action of the cat eating - the fish was eaten by the cat.

Although use of the passive voice is discouraged by English teaching, the Japanese passive mode is common – it shifts the emphasis from who did it to who it was done to.

If-then

If-then, usually called the *ba* or hypothetical form, is a condition of the form "if X is true, then Y is true" (*e.g.,* If it rains, I will go inside).

$$S\ ga\ V1\ ba\ V2$$
If subject S does V1 then V2 will happen

Example

(watashi)	*(ga)*	*kusuri*	*o*	*nome*	*ba*	*(watashi)*	*(ga)*	*naoru*
(I)		medicine		drink	if	(I)		recover
Subject		Dir Obj		Verb		Subject		Verb

If I drink my medicine, I will recover

If-Once (*ra*) is used to describe a situation that has a one-time result or an actual result. The verb in the If sentence must be past tense, with any auxiliary ending in *ta*. For this reason, this form is usually called the *tara* form. It is really the *ra* form, the *ta* belonging to the previous key.

You can change to the if-then form if the result is actual, or to the If-then form if the result is hypothetical.

(anata)	*(ga)*	*Nihon*	*ni*	*ki*	*ta*	*ra*
(you)		Japan to		come	did	if
Subject		Adverb		Verb		

If you go to Japan

(anata)	*(ga)*	*sakura*	*o*	*mira*	*reru*
(you)		cherry blossoms		see	can
Subject		Dir Obj		Verb	

You can see cherry blossoms

If-Context (*nara*) is used in the context of some situation: "I want to go to Nagasaki" – "If you go to Nagasaki I go too".

Example

The Context

anata	wa		*(anata)*	*(ga)*	*Nagoya*	*ni*	*iku*	*nara*
As for you			(you)		Nagoya to		go	if
Topic			Subject		Adverb		Verb	

if you go to Nagoya . . .

The Response

Watashi	mo		*(Watashi)*	*(mo)*	*Nagoya*	*ni*	*isi*	*masu*
As for Me	also		(I)	(also)	Nagoya	to	go	do
Topic			Subject		Adverb		Verb	

I too Nagoya (will) go

If-Always (*to*) is used to relate a situation in which the result is given – always the same. For instance "If I drop a rock, it will fall". *to* meansand: If X happens **and** Y happens (as a result)".

ame	*ga*	*furu*	*to*		*suzushiku*	*naru*
rain		fall **and**			cool	get
Subject		Verb			Adverb	Verb

If it rains, I will get wet

Command

Avoid using this mode. It is used mostly by police or parents with their children, and on public road signs (*e.g.,* Stop). It should only be used for emergencies when, for instance, there is no time for being polite. The sentence format is

S *ga* I **ni** D o V
Subject S commands/asks indirect object I to do Direct Object D

Example

otōsan	*ga*	*Kōta*	*ni*	*shukudai*	*o*	*shi*	*ro*	*to*	*itta*
Father		*Kōta*	to	homework		do	!	quote	said
Subject		Indir Obj		Dir Obj		Verb		Verb	

Father said to Kōta "do homework"

Comparison Sentences

This bag is cheap more than that bag. This is a description sentence, of the form "A has the property B".

Comparison sentences are used to compare two items, such as A is more C (something) than B.

hō means 'side of comparison': *kaban no hō* means bag's side of comparison. The *no* in "noun *no hō*" is possessive, meaning "noun's *hō*, or "noun's side of the comparison".

kaku **yori**	*yomu koto no* **hō ga**	**suki** *desu*
Adverb	Subject	Copula
writing than	reading's side of comparison	likable is

Reading is (more) likeable than writing
i.e., I like reading more than writing
Note that reading (*yomu*) is changed to a noun by adding *koto*

Comparison – A *no* hō *ga* C: A's alternative is more C

kono kaban no hō ga	*yasui desu*
This bag's side of comparison	cheap is
Subject	Copula

This bag is cheaper (than others)

Comparison - A is more C than B

kono kaban no hō ga	sono kaban yori	yasui desu
Subject	Adverb	Copula
This bag's alternative	that bag more than	cheap is

This bag is cheaper than that bag.

Description Sentences

Descriptions Sentences have no action. The present some property of the subject. The property may be an attribute or state of being. The use a copula element instead of a verb element.

		Does to		
		Indirect Object		
Introduction	Whose property	Does with	Property	Ending
Topic	Subject	Direct Object	Copula	Tag
		Does how		
		Adverb		

- The optional topic element is an introduction to the sentence. It is grammatically separate from the sentence.

- The mandatory subject element is the thing or person whose property is being related. Even though it is mandatory, it is often a virtual subject - understood but not written or said.

- The optional indirect object element is seldom used.

- The optional direct object element is seldom used.

- The optional adverb elements are seldom used.

- The mandatory copula element describes the property of the subject.

- The optional tag element describes the mood of the sentence or connects the sentence to another or defines the sentence as a question.

Example sentences

Attribute Sentence

An attribute sentence provides a description of an attribute of the subject.

<u>Example</u>

watashi no kuruma	*wa*		*(watashi no kuruma)*	*(ga)*	*midori*	*desu*
As for my car			(My car)		Subaru	is
Topic			Subject		Copula	

My car is a Subaru

Negative Attribute Sentence

A negative attribute sentence describes an attribute that the subject does not have.

watashi no kuruma	*wa*		*(watashi no kuruma)*	*(ga)*	*Doitsu no*	*de wa*	*ari*	*masen*
As for my car			(My car)		German	as for being	Is	not
Topic			Subject		Copula			

My car is not German

Existence Sentences

An existence sentence states that the subject exists.

Ocha	*wa*		*(ocha)*	*(ga)*	*aru*
As for tea			(tea)		Is
Topic			Subject		Copula

Tea exists (there is tea)

ashita	*watashi*	*wa*		*(watashi)*	*(ga)*	*Hokkaido*	*ni*	*i*	*masu*
tomorrow	As for me			(I)		Hokkaido	in		be
Adverb	Topic			Subject		Copula			

Tomorrow I Hokkaido in (will) be
Tomorrow I will be in Hokkaido

inu	wa	(inu)	(ga)	uchi no naka ni	ari	masu
As fir (the) dog		dog		house's inside at	Is	
Topic		Subject		Copula		

The dog is in the house

On-going state of existence

Miho san	wa	(Miho san)	(ga)	hanashite	i	masu
As for Miho		Miho		talk	ing	is
Topic		Subject		Copula		

Miho is talking

Negative state of existence

Midori san	wa	(Midor sani)	(ga)	nemute	i	masen
Midori		(Midori)		sleep	ing	not
Topic		Subject		Copula		

Midori is not sleeping

Natsuki san	wa	(Natsuk sai)	(ga)	tabe	masen
Natsuki		Natsuki		eat	not
Topic		Subject		Copula	

Natsuki does not eat

Combining Sentences

Tags

Tags are words appended to the sentence. Question tags and continuation tags are part of the sentence. Mood tags are not part of the sentence; they contain information about the sentence.

Questions are exactly like statements; except they have a Question Tag appended.

Kai san	*wa*
Kai	
Topic Element	

(Kai san)	*(ga)*	*nihonjin*	*desu*
Kai		Japanese is	
Subject Element		Copula Element	

(Statement) Kai is Japanese

Kai san	*wa*
Kai	
Topic Element	

(Kai san)	*(ga)*	*nihonjin*	*desu*
Kai		Japanese is	
Subject Element		Copula Element	

ka
?
Tag Element

(Question) Is Kai Japanese?

Linking Sentences

Sometimes one wants to run two or more related sentences together. Other times, one is using conditional sentences – If X is true then Y is true, which involves two sentences.

Linking two Sentences

Two related sentences can be linked.

te form - Linking two sentences is accomplished by using the *te* form of the main verb of the first Sentence.

<u>Example</u>

watashi	wa		(watashi)	(ga)	Kōbe	ni	i	**tte**	sarōinsutēki	o	tabe	mashita
As for me			(I)		Kōbe to			went (and)	sirloin steak		eat did	
Topic Element			Subject Element		Adverb Element		Verb Element		Dir Obj Element		Verb Element	

I went to Kōbe and ate sirloin steak.

Descriptive Sentences can also be linked in the same way.

<u>Example</u>

tenki	wa		(tenki)	(ga)	atsuku	**te**	amegachi	desu
As for the weather			(weather)		hot is (and)		rainy is	
Topic Element			Subject Element		Copula Element		Copula Element	

The weather is hot and rainy.

de is the *te* form of *da.*

<u>*Linking with Tag*</u>

Sentences can also be linked with a Tag word.

soshite (and)

watashi	wa		(watashi)	(ga)	sushi	o	tabe	mashita		soshite
As for me			(I)		sushi		eat did			and
Topic Element			Subject Element		DirObj Element		Verb Element			Tag Element

I ate sushi and . . .

(watashi)	(ga)	osake	o	nomi	mashita
(I)		sake		drink did	
Subject Element		DirObj Element		Verb Element	

I drank sake.

demo (but)

Atsushi san	wa
As for Aysushi	
Topic	

(Atsushi dan)	(ga)	terebi	o	mi	tai
(Atsushi san)		television		watch want	
Subject		DirObj		Verb	

demo
but
Tag

I want to watch television but . . .

(watashi)	(ga)	nemui	desu
(I)		sleepy am	
Subject		Copula	

I am sleepy.

node (so)

watashi	wa
As for me	
Topic	

(watashi)	(ga)	Ju go sai	na
(I)		15 years old	
Subject		Adverb	

node
so
Tag

I am 15 years old, so . . .

(watashi)	(ga)	osake	o	nomi	masen
(I)		sake		drink not	
Subject		DirObj		Verb	

I do not drink sake.

Other Tag word Connectors

kara (therefore)
noni (despite)
tamel (because)

Conditional Sentences

Every language has a way of saying "if X is true then Y is true". However, Japanese has several forms of conditional sentences that have slightly different meanings.

If-Then (*ba*) is used for hypothetical conditions, *i.e.*, those where the possibility of occurring is unknown:" If I will the lottery, I will be rich". The If-Then form is a general-purpose conditional statement. Unlike the following forms, it has no assumptions or embedded meanings.

(watashi)	(ga)	kusuri	o	nome	**ba**
(I))		medicine		drink **if**	
Subject		Dir Obj		Verb	

(watashi)	(ga)	naoru
(I)		recover
Subject		Verb

If I drink medicine

I will recover.

If-Once (*ra*) is used to describe a situation that has a one-time result or an actual result. The Verb in the If sentence must be past tense, with a Helper ending in *ta*. For this reason, this form is usually called the *tara* form.

You can change to the If-then form if the result is actual, or to the If-then form if the result is hypothetical.

(anata)	(ga)	Nihon	ni	ki	ta	**ra**
(you)		Japan to		come **if**		
Subject		Adverb		Verb		

(anata)	(ga)	sakura	o	mira	reru
(you)		cherry blossoms		see can	
Subject		Dir Obj		Verb	

If you come to Japan

you can see the cherry blossoms.

If-Context (*nara*) is used in the context of some situation: "I want to go to Nagasaki" –"If you go to Nagasaki, I will also go", "If you are cold, close the window".

The Context

watashi	wa,
As for me,	
Topic	

(watash)	(ga)	Nagoya	ni	iki	masu
(I)		Nagoya to		go	
Subject		Adverb		Verb	

I go to Nagoya.

The Response

anata	wa
you	
Topic	

(anata)	(ga)	Nagoya	ni	iku	**nara**
(you)		Nagoya to		go if	
Subject		Adverb		Verb	

If you go to Nagoya,

watashi	mo
I also	
Topic	

(watashi)	(mo)	iku
(I)		go
Subject		Verb

I go too.

If-Always (*to*) is used to relate a situation in which the result is given – always the same. For instance, "If I drop a rock, it will fall". *to* means 'and':" X happens, **and** Y happens (as a result)".

ame	ga	furu	**to**
rain		fall **and**	
Subject		Verb	

suzushiku	naru
cool	get
Adverb	Verb

If rain falls, it will get cool.

Comparison Sentences

Comparison sentences are used to compare two items, such as A is more something than C.

hō means 'side of comparison': *kaban no hō* = bag's side of comparison.

The *no* in Noun *no* hō *is possessive,* meaning Noun's *hō,* or Noun's side of the comparison. It is not required for verb comparison: *hachiru hō* – run's side of comparison.

*kaku **yori**   yomu **hō ga**   suki desu*

Adverb   Subject   Copula

writing than   reading side   likable is

Reading is (more) likeable than writing

i.e., I like reading more than writing

Comparison – *A no hō ga C: A's alternative is more C*

kono kaban no hō ga	*yasui desu*
Subject	Copula
This bag's side of comparison	cheap is

This bag is cheap (er than other bags)

Comparison - *A is more C than B*

kono kaban no hō ga	*sono kaban yori*	*yasui desu*
Subject	Adverb	Copula
This bag's alternative	that bag more than	cheap is

This bag is cheap more than that bag

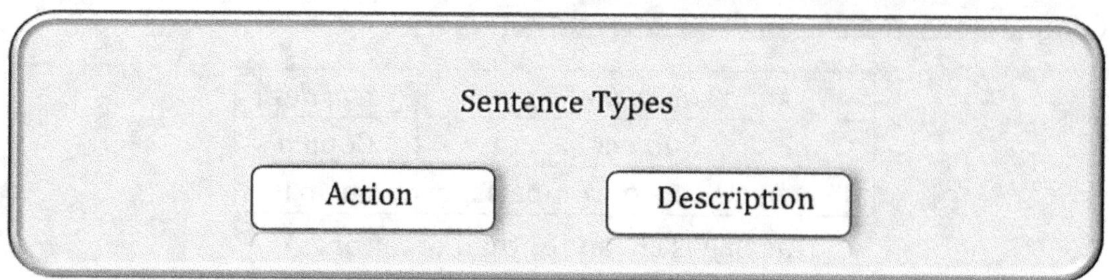

Takeaways

Sentences are assemblies of elements.

There are two types of sentences:

Action sentences describe an action of the subject. The action is defined by the verb element. The direct object defines what is used to perform the action, and the indirect object defines the recipient of the action. Adverbs modify the verb.

Description sentences describe some property of the subject. The property may be color, size, ownership, citizenship, *etc.,* or it may be a state of being:

an ongoing action, such as running,
or a state of existence, such as location.

Sentences may be linked using the *te* form.

Sentences citing conditions (if X then Y) are linked by conditional verb forms.